LIVING WITH A
SNOW(WO)MAN

How do you deal with a death sentence being given to a loved one with the diagnosis of a disease? This is one such story.

This book is dedicated to my wife: Carol; our children: Christi, Kimberly, David, Stephani, Patrick, and Bailey; Carol's mother and sister: Marlen and Karen – I love you all and thank you for being there. Also, to any and all that have been diagnosed with an alphabet disease or have lost a loved one to one. I wish you all the best.

Introduction

I want to take a moment to set the tone. I would like you, the reader, to know what I am trying to do with this book. Since I first published the original blog posts chronicling my wife's journey with MSA I have been told; "you should write a book!". Well, recommendation taken – I am writing a book.

The bulk of this book will be reprints of the blog posts that I did/have done during and after my wife's diagnosis and subsequent death from her "alphabet disease" (more to come on that) – MSA, Multiple System Atrophy. I will not go into detail here explaining what that is as I hope the blog posts will do so. I then am going to try to do an explanation of where I was "at" during that time frame as well as speak somewhat for my wife's state of mind (forgive me Carol, I hope I get it somewhat right! Speaking of that – my wife's name is/was Carol, I will refer to her that way throughout this book.)

This book and the included blog posts will take you from the beginnings of the disease symptoms to after Carol's demise. There are a lot of moments that are obviously raw as I started this blog primarily as an outlet for me. I sometimes can express myself in the written word better than with the spoken one. There may be errors, especially in syntax and grammar. If they occur in the dialogue and additions now, I am sorry. I will do my best to make this readable and correct. However, I am not doing a grammar lesson or a writing class. If the mistakes occur in the reprints of the blog posts, even if I catch them now, I will leave them as I feel they may help show my/our state of mind at the time.

This book is dedicated to Carol and her memory, as well as to my six children. Two of our daughters were instrumental in her day to day care as I kept working full-time to pay the bills. We literally could not have done it without them. These two and the others were all faced with a mother diagnosed with a fatal illness at a relatively young age –

Carol was showing symptoms at 51 and diagnosed at 52. They then had to face the loss of their mother at the age of 56. This book also is dedicated to the memory of all those that have and are suffering with this terrible illness. MSA is a killer from which there is no remission and no escape. I wish the best to all those family members that have had to face a similar journey. A portion of any funds earned from this book will be given to MSA research in the hopes that someday there will be treatments and possibly a cure.

As mentioned above, the blog posts will be printed here verbatim as they are/were in the blog. If you would like to visit the blog however, it can be found at www.livingiwithasnowman.blogspot.com. Even after all this time, and me not updating posts much at all, the site still gets hundreds and hundreds of visits a month. I still get emails and comments in the blog from family members and patients that have questions or just to offer a thought about what I have written. Some offer solace and best wishes for Carol, myself, or our family. I try to acknowledge and respond to all of them, and plan to continue to do so the best of my ability in the future. If I can offer any help or answer any question for someone going through what this disease can do, I am more than glad to do so.

CHAPTER ONE

THE START

My blogging started as an outlet for me to express myself and to chronicle the journey that we were on. I originally did a blog with these comments on Carol and her disease mixed in. That blog is still active at www.justsomeposts.blogspot.com. I realized rather quickly that the posts concerning Carol and MSA deserved their own forum and platform. That is how the Living with a Snow(wo)man blog – www.livingwithasnowman.blogspot.com - came about. Although not the first post I did, this is the post that I started the blog with. I think it explains itself. You may note there are two dates on most of the blog posts. The dates in red with the title are the dates that the original post was made on the first blog. The other date is when it was posted to the new blog.

Wednesday, February 3, 2010

A new forum - the timeline and setup

I thought I would do this post to keep my other blog http://www.justsomeposts.blogspot.com/ "clean" with my ridiculous thoughts and political/social commentary. This blog will be my thoughts and comments on my and my wife's journey with her disease - multiple system atrophy. If you are not familiar with this disease, don't feel bad. We still have to explain it to doctors, nurses and medical staff most places we go. Google it, you will find good information out there. Here is the official definition from the **National Institutes of Health:**

Multiple System Atrophy (MSA) is a progressive neurodegenerative disorder characterized by symptoms of autonomic nervous system failurs such as fainting spells and bladder control problems, combined with motor control symptoms such as tremor, rigidity, and loss of motor coordination. MSA affects both men and women primarily in their 50s.

There is no cure for MSA. Currently, there are no treatments to delay the progress of neurodegeneration in the brain. But there are treatments to help people cope with some of the more disabling symptoms of MSA.

The disease tends to advance rapidly over the course of 9 to 10 years, with progressive loss of motor skills, eventual confinement to bed, and death. There is no remission from the disease. There is currently no cure.

Why "Living with a Snow(wo)man" you may ask? I liken this disease to a "melting" of the individual. Trying to hang on to the loved one you knew is akin to trying to keep a snowman (or snowwoman in our case) whole. The disease is insidious. Watching the progress is like watching a snowman melt. Hence the title.

This blog will be mostly for me. I will try to not be too morbid or self-serving, but hey - MY BLOG! If you want to follow along, you are welcomed. If there are things you like or dislike, tell me. If you think I should not be doing it, or hate it; don't read it. Again - MY BLOG. One thing I am NOT looking for is pity or empathy for me. Although this disease is a trial for me and affects every aspect of my life (whether as the elephant in the room, or just the day to day scheduling), the burden on me is nothing compared to the burden on my wife. If you need to offer pity, empathy, sorrow, prayers, or tears; offer them to her. She is facing the disease with a character, bravery, and dignity that I probably could not muster on a bet.

After this opening, the first posts will be "reprints" of the posts I have done on my other blog. Some of them may not be "clean" posts just about the disease. The new posts will be that, but I want a chronicle of where we've been. First a timeline and an update of where we are today.

Sept 2005 - my wife called me at work and told me she had felt ill trying to get in the door of our house. She said she could not get the key to work and felt disoriented and dizzy. I thought she had had a "mini-stroke"(TIA) and told her to take an aspirin, a vitamin E, and to sit down and wait for me. I went home and took her to the ER. After hours of testing, they determined that she may indeed have had an transient ischemic event. We were told to go home and rest. More testing followed. We are not sure what if any relationship this event had in her present state, but we always start our timeline here when we talk to doctors (and there have been a LOT of those!).

My wife for years and years had told me she would get "dizzy" when walking from a parking lot in the daytime into a store or mall. We thought nothing of it, but mentioned it to the doctor when she had her suspected TIA. During the months following her TIA she would get dizzy and light-headed upon standing, especially after sitting a long time. Going from an air-conditioned space (a car particularly) to a hot parking lot was especially bad. She then started experiencing syncope (fainting) upon standing or exertion. She started going to doctors. This is all in the early months of 2006. She was still working full time as a registered nurse, driving, cooking, and otherwise leading a fairly normal life. She just passed out from time to time. She went to cardiologists, endocrinologists, and neurologists; as well as her family doctor. After tests and tests and tests, where she was pronounced a "very healthy woman except that you have this syncope going on", we found a doctor that gave her a diagnosis of MSA in early 2007. However, I left out the progression of symptoms.

During 2006 her fainting spells progressively got worse. She could tell they were coming on most of the time, but could not do anything to prevent them. She passed out in the parking lot walking into work a few times. They never told her directly, but we heard she was suspected of being an alcoholic or drug addict by many. She suffered from a loss of coordination as well as some vision problems. By June of 2006 she was out of work. She was told that she was too much of a liability. That was a big milestone for her. Losing one's profession is to lose one's self in our society, to a point. She was using a cane to help with her balance by mid to late 2006. I was accompanying her to the doctors now, as her driving was not as good; and our concern that something serious was going on had definitely set in. We went to many, many doctors; none who could offer any answers.

At UNC Hospitals in February of 2007 (my wife says January, but I am writing this and I remember February) Dr. Georgia Lea gave us the official diagnosis of MSA. I had reached that conclusion from studies on the internet and we had discussed it some in general; but unless you have had it happen to you, you cannot imagine getting a diagnosis like that. A death sentence - no cure, no treatment, no hope. That was a rough day. She made phone calls and we met with our kids and told them. A lot of tears were shed that day.

Back to my wife's symptoms. She had developed Parkinson's like tremors during the latter months of 2006 and into 2007. MSA is considered one of the class of diseases sometimes called "Parkinson's Plus" (it's the "plus" that gets you) and this is part of the progression of the disease.
Treatment with Carbidopa/Levadopa started to help with these. She remains on the drug today.
There are also some drugs that can be taken to help with the syncope. The problem with her is if there was a negative side effect from a drug, she seemed to get it. But, through study and experience we became good a mitigating if not stopping the fainting spells.
During this time her handwriting became very small and somewhat illegible. This too is a common symptom. Her speech has also suffered with some slurring occurring by this time.

Sometime in early to mid 2007 she went to a walker, or more accurately - a rollator (a walker with wheel instead of skids). She was still moving pretty well, but needed it for balance - which was deteriorating. By December of 2007 she went to using a wheelchair most of the time. By early 2008, the wheelchair was full-time. The symptoms mentioned above were all still around, and more pronounced. Her writing was almost illegible even to her. She would write something down and days later have no idea what it said. During 2008 she was using a powerchair for getting out and about some as well as the wheelchair.

In 2009, the symptoms continued to worsen. Her speech was slurring more and more. Phone conversations, even with those that know her became more difficult. The ability to take steps is waning as her reliance on the chair increases. The tremors are more pronounced and make eating difficult. During this time, she went from needing her food cut up to needing help getting it on to her silverware, to needing help eating.

Today, my wife is in her wheelchair, lift chair, or bed all the time. We do get out some, in fact we did a cruise last October. Her ability to write is pretty much gone. Her ability to eat unaided is pretty much gone. Her ability to hold a conversation on the phone is pretty much gone. Her ability to type is pretty much gone. Her tremors are very pronounced and annoying. Her balance is non-existent. You get the picture.

Now for the good(?). Her ability to laugh is still there. Her ability to make me laugh is still there. We try to have a good laugh every day. I do my best to make her laugh as she does me. Her mind is still there (that can be good and bad, she definitely realizes what she has lost and where she is headed). Her memory is still better than mine on certain things. The love she has for her children, grandchildren, and family is boundless. She is one of the most selfless individuals I have ever known. Her concern for others, especially her family far outweighs her concern for herself. I am reminded every day why I married her. I am reminded every day why this disease is a living hell for both of us.

On with the show. As I said the next posts will be "reprints" of posts I have made on my wife and her disease on my other blog.

Posted by gumbypoole aka Scott Poole at 8:49 AM

The next posts will be presented chronologically in order as I originally posted them to my first blog.

I am going to try to set the tone for each on with a short preface and then comment after the post where I feel I can add something relevant.

CHAPTER TWO

ALPHABET DISEASES

This is the actual first post I did on my blog prior to me putting them together and posting all new thoughts in the "Snow(wo)man" blog. It was a start and where I first wanted to let people know that there are diseases out there so terrible, complex, and unknown, that we just use initials to reference them. I was frustrated and a bit afraid.

Wednesday, February 3, 2010

Alphabet diseases - originally written 11/13/07

I have unfortunately learned over the past year about a segment of medicine that I would have rather not. That segment is what I call the alphabet diseases. When you go to the doctor with a complaint or problems you are looking for a diagnosis and then a treatment and/or cure. What you do not want is a diagnosis and a pat on the back. The latter is what seems to happen with the alphabet diseases.

What are the alphabet diseases, you ask? You are aware of some of them such as MS, MD, and ALS. These are terrible diseases in their own right with prognoses that are not good. However, I have learned of others that are as bad and/or worse due to the lack of knowledge and information available. How would you like a disease that when you are seeing medical staff for the first time have to be told what the disease is. Blank stares or mumbles signify a lack of understanding for what the jumble of letters you just threw out mean. Two of these alphabet diseases that I have some personal knowledge of now are MSA (Multiple System Atrophy) and PSP (Progressive Supernuclear Palsy). These are both diseases that have a terrible prognosis and worse than that, no treatment or cures! Not only that, but as I said above they are almost unknown in the medical world as well.

MSA is such a rare and "orphaned" disease that the national support organization had to cancel the plans for the annual meeting due to lack of funds. They have no spokesperson or telethon, like I said they can't even get support for an annual convention. PSP does have a Patricia Richardson (of Tool Time fame) fame as a spokesperson due to her father dying of the disease, but again -ask most medical people what it is and wait for the stammering to begin.

I started this two days ago and have been interrupted twice. I have lost my original thoughts and fervor for the subject. Basically, it is a warning that you do not want to hear a diagnosis with an alphabet disease in it.

G'Day

Posted by gumbypoole aka Scott Poole at 9:50 PM

It was a start. Although reading it now I cringe at the lack of knowledge I showed, it did show some of the frustration we felt as Carol's disease progressed. It is hard for someone that has not gone through it to know what it is like to go to a doctor and be told you are dying, and also being told – "OK, we will see you in six months". We are so used to medical miracles and drugs that can help with almost any disease, most of us do not think of the thousands upon thousands that are afflicted with a disease with no treatment.

CHAPTER THREE

FRUSTRATION MOUNTS

As I mentioned previously, one of the things that have to be learned and accepted is MSA and other alphabet diseases have no real treatment and are terminal. Yes, there are drugs that can help with the symptoms. There are physical "tricks" that can be learned to mitigate some of the problems and issues that arise. However, there is always the hopelessness that comes from seeing six specialists and being told – "You are going to die". (to be fair, although most of the Neurologists we met had the bedside manner of a fence post, none were that blunt)

Thursday, February 4, 2010

Questions - originally posted 1/20/2008

There are two blogs that I have been thinking of writing for a while. This is one of them.

What do you say to a person you love and have lived with for over three decades when they turn to you and say with tears in their eyes, "I don't want to die"?

What do you do when you have kids and family members that just ask "How is she doing?" and just want to hear "Fine", or "About the same"; even if it is not true?

How do you make people understand that you are living with it every day and that it is not going away and that it is hard? Hard for those of us around her, but even harder for her.

How can you watch your wife of thirty-four plus years not able to get out of bed or up a single step unassisted when you still see her as the eighteen-year-old you married?

How do you answer a 53-year-old that asks you if she will see her daughter, a junior, graduate from high school?

How do you get your kids to get off their asses and recognize their mother needs them? (with one exception, Steph) Not later, NOW!

How do you respond to a social security ruling that denies disability, so your insurance is going up to more than your rent every month? How do you deal with insurance and government people that are on a timetable that is slower than a glacier?

What do you do to help when you have seen, in eleven months, a progression from walking slowly, to walking with a cane, to a rollator/walker sometimes - cane sometimes, to a rollator / walker all the time, to a wheelchair sometimes?

How do you convince someone to go out when every movement is a tremendous effort and one of your biggest fears is seeing someone you know or used to work with?

What do you do when you are a control freak and things are out of your control, no matter how hard you try?

I do NOT want any sympathy for me. I am not going to say I am not human. I am not going to say this was not a release for me. But comments on my condition are irrelevant. Sympathy, compassion, concern, and love for my wife is demanded. She needs all of you.

Questions need answering. I don't have the answers.

Posted by gumbypoole aka Scott Poole at 2:38 PM

Obviously, at this point I am very, very frustrated and my wife is beyond that and into depression. The questions I listed above were constant. The tears shed were real, and reminders that we have no guarantee of tomorrow. There were some wonderful medical personnel - doctors, nurses, and therapists — that made things livable. But the questions and lack of answers were maddening.

CHAPTER FOUR

REALIZATION I NEED A NEW BLOG

Remember, I was still posting these within the body of my "all-purpose" blog at www.justsomeposts.blogspot.com. A lot of the posts were (and are today) an attempt at humor. When I have a comical post and then segue into a serious somewhat morbid one, I was told it was causing problems. I cannot remember which of my children said it, but someone called me after the previous post was up and asked me to warn them as they started crying at work/school when they read it. So, I decided to put a warning in the title.

Friday, February 5, 2010
A serious one - originally posted April 6,2008
If you have not read the first post in this blog - please do so. All this is based around the first post.

I wanted to do a blog on perspective. Life and our evaluation of it is based a LOT on perspective. I got a great example of this yesterday.

My wife is disabled!! Officially. Perspective - - -

On face value, that would not appear to be a good thing. Disability is not to be cheered. Ah, official disability is (or can be). My seventeen-year-old was here yesterday when my wife opened the letter and we were cheering for disability. She made a comment that is was weird that we were happy with Mom being disabled. I explained we weren't, but...

My wife's condition is affected not one bit by what the doctors, bureaucrats, or anyone else labels it. She is no more nor no less disabled or ill than prior to getting the letter. However, getting the letter signifies official legal acceptance of her disability. That will hopefully lead to a lessening of the financial burdens of her condition and let us deal exclusively with the physical ones.

I think I mentioned before how during the diagnosis stage, my wife and I found ourselves cheering and wishing for a diagnosis of MS or Parkinson's. Not to say both of those diseases are not horrific and life changing in their own right, but... Perspective - - -

The other diagnosis we were faced with was of a magnitude worse - MSA. I wrote a blog a while back about the alphabet diseases. The addition of an "A" to "M" and "S" takes a horrible disease and makes it imminently more horrible.

In our discussions about disease and disability my wife commented on her possibility of having MS and/or Parkinson's. I said, "I know I was pulling for you to have one of them as well." That caused another comment from my daughter about how we were weird. I had to explain to her it is all about perspective.

Let's have a round of applause for my wife's official disability. From anyone else's perspective that may sound strange. From here it is receiving a standing ovation.
Posted by gumbypoole aka Scott Poole at 4:51 PM

Although not a rant per se, I did want to start warning folks that I was going serious. I also was thinking more and more about a separate blog for this subject.

CHAPTER FIVE

MORE FRUSTRATION

I can feel and viscerally remember the frustration I was feeling at this time. I am not sure how well I was treating the rest of the world at this point, so to any and all I may have offended – I am sorry!

Carol's physical decline was accelerating and increasing. The frustration for all of us was immense. I think this may be mentioned in a later post, but this is also about the time that she told me "she just would like to have a break – to get away from the disease for a time." Then she added "maybe not, it would be too horrible to go back to this again.

Saturday, February 6, 2010

Even More Questions - originally posted July 30, 2008

You may get this more if you read (or re-read) these older posts: (which are now contained below - read the first post in this blog to get the drift)

"A Serious One" from 4/6/08

"Alphabet diseases" from 11/13/07 and

"Questions" from 1/20/08

I am still trying to get answers to the Questions asked in the post above. I have not found any that are worthy of printing. I have come up with more questions:

How does one handle seeing the continual decline of their spouse and not being able to do a thing about it?

How do you take the inability of your 53-year-old wife to get out of bed, or in and out of the shower unaided?

How do you answer questions that beg not to be asked, like: will I see Bailey (our daughter, a rising senior) graduate; will Hannah (our granddaughter - almost 3) remember me; or will I see Landon (or grandson - 6 months) walk?

How do you comfort your bride of 35+ years when she looks at you with tears streaming down her face?

Most of all, how do you offer support and help when you are so damn mad at the world and the situation that all you want to do is scream!? When even your best efforts just don't cut it. When nothing at all makes it go away!?! When the best that doctors can do is "See you in three months".

If you are diagnosed with cancer; even one of the terrible ones, there are treatments and a chance of recovery or remission. Most cancers now have a good recovery rate. (before anyone with cancer takes offense, I am not making light of cancer, just comparisons) She does not get that. We get a gradual, progressive march downhill, with nothing to assist or offer hope.

55 is not a time to be facing the death of a spouse. There is never a good time, but with a known life expectancy in this country of well over 70+, a few decades more might have helped. 53 is definitely not the time to be facing ones own death. As frustrating as this time is for me, I cannot fathom what it must be like to be on the other side of this.

This disease is like the elephant in the room. Everyone can see it, everyone has his or her reaction to it; no one comments on it.

Our kids have stepped it up since the "Questions" post of above. I still get asked "How is your wife?" from people that just want to hear - O.K. or at worst - "about the same". I appreciate the thought (when asked sincerely, not conversationally), I just get weary of the answer.

Down enough yet? I know I am.

Comments welcomed, support for my wife - demanded.

I cannot speak for everyone, but I will say if you know of someone that is suffering from a disease, sometimes what they want is acknowledgement but then to be treated like themselves. Carol refused to see her former co-workers or friends as she told me she hated the way everyone treated her – like she was broken. Sometimes acknowledging the elephant and then moving on around it is the right answer! One of the real issues with this disease, like so many others of the central nervous system/brain, is that the patient feels "normal" inside. The body does not work correctly; speech, writing, and any movement is compromised. But the part of the mind that is the individual is still there. That was one thing that Carol and I tried to do every day – laugh. She had a great sense of humor and loved to laugh. Even facing death, she loved to laugh. So, we did; whenever we could.

Wow, sometimes I did cry out for just me. I had forgotten this one. Again, the frustration at not being able to do anything was horrible. This one speaks for itself.

Monday, February 8, 2010

A Three Hour Tour, or, Perchance to Drown - originally published 12/2/2008

Imagine you and your spouse, or significant other, are on a nice boat ride called life. You are on this inconceivably large boat in a sea of unimaginable size on a trip of indeterminate length. Once in a while, you go through some beautiful. almost indescribable days where birds sing, wonderful angelic music accompanies you in your daily activities, and everything you want is there before you. Then there are the dark and stormy days where all you can do is hold on to the rail and upchuck your lunch into the water. Most of the days, however, are just a boat ride.

One day your spouse falls overboard, fully clothed, and for no apparent reason. You quickly toss them a line, and say "hold on, I'll get you out!" There is no reason to panic, people fall into the water all the time. Plus, they are a fairly strong swimmer, we will get them out. So, you start pulling on the rope. After pulling and pulling you notice they are not any closer to the boat. You decide you need help.

You go and get the some of the lifeguards that are stationed around the boat. One by one they examine the situation. All of them, after careful thought and deep reflection based on years of training, say "They are in the water. They will surely drown. All we can do is keep them on the line from the boat and wait." You become more and more agitated and upset. You go and get one lifeguard after another. Some haven't got a clue. All the rest just say, "At some unpredictable time in the future they will drown. Keep them nourished, provide fresh water, and here is a wonder drug in case they get cramps."

You consider going into the water yourself. However, there is no good way to get in, and definitely no way out. So, you sit by the rail and talk to your loved one about the good days where the birds sang, angelic music accompanied you, and all was before you. Meanwhile, it becomes harder and harder for your spouse to keep their head above the water. One of your greatest fears is a storm coming up and causing waves that they surely could not ride out. More and more time is spent just working to keep their head above the water. Meanwhile, you can only sit and watch.

Enjoy your cruise.

I will combine this post with the above as six or seven weeks later I was on a similar thought plane:

DRIVE - originally posted 1/18/2009

Imagine you are out for a drive. You are motoring along. Occasionally you stop to get a bite to eat or to enjoy some of the sites. But mostly you are cruising and taking in the ride.

Suddenly you realize your vehicle is going on it's own. Not too fast, not too slow, but ever moving whether you want it to or not. You realize you are not really even steering the car or choosing the exact direction you are travelling any longer. You run red lights and stop signs. You pass in no passing zones and are passed in others. But, you continue relentlessly forward. There is no reverse.

You would love to just STOP, to pull in somewhere and sit and take in the local flavor. You know, however, the only stopping you will be doing is by crashing or just running out of gas somewhere you don't want to be.

But, maybe moving towards SOMETHING is better than stopping at NOTHING.

Welcome to our life.

Carol was dealing with this, at least outwardly, better at this point than I was, I think. The frustration and dismay at the lack of control over our lives was definitely in abundance, as shown in these two posts. I truly wish that none of us ever had to deal with a situation like this, but I know many people are and do, unfortunately too large a number. Receiving a diagnosis that your loved one (or yourself) has an incurable, untreatable, and 100% fatal illness is hard to imagine unless you have been there. I say again to all of you that are going through this or have gone through this; bless you.

CHAPTER SEVEN

PRACTICALITIES

There are few things that all we of the human race have in common. We are all born – at different times, places, and conditions; but all born. We all share time, I like to say that one of the very few things that humans have in complete equality is time. 24 hours in a day is all we have and all we get. The good news is; no one gets less. The richest and the poorest among us are all the same. The final thing we all share is death. As it is jokingly said: "no one gets out of this alive!". So true, death is inevitable.

One other thing we all share is bodily functions. I will not take this to the level of an explanation (at least not beyond what is contained in the post below), but we all must do "our business" as it is sometimes referred to. Being wheelchair bound and dependent on others for assistance in movement limits the capacity and capability to perform these necessary functions as we are used to doing – alone and in a timely manner, in most cases.

Carol and I continued to try to do the things we/she (with emphasis on she) wanted. After her diagnosis and well after she was confined to a wheelchair full-time we travelled. We took three cruises, we would visit her mother in central Florida on several occasions, and some other less lengthy journeys. Travel means being away from the routine and "accessories" a wheelchair bound individual has become accustom to having to assist with these necessary functions. One of the biggest issues we had when travelling was finding a bathroom that we could use with her, the wheelchair, and myself. Sometimes a large portion of a trip was spent looking for and then using the bathroom. I can tell you there were times we commandeered the women's or men's restroom with a quickly deputized assistant to handle the issue. Here is one I wrote during one of our trips to central Florida. A note: to all those that have and are installing "family restrooms", three cheers. These were few and far between nine years ago, at least where we were travelling. They are a GREAT boon to anyone in a similar situation to ours as well as families travelling with small children. Kudos!

To Pee or not to Pee (with apologies to the Bard) - originally posted 3-12-09

I know a lot of people are crying the blues today over the economy (and justifiably so in a lot of cases). However, you have all heard the statement made - "at least you've got your health", probably a million times. If you "have your health" and have remained relatively healthy, you probably ignore the statement or mumble a "yeah" and move on.

The process of waste elimination is a pretty basic need. If you remember basic biology - taking in food and elimination of waste were signs of biological life. If you are a human, the waste elimination process has taken leaps of societal and hygienic improvements from Og and his lot heading for the other side of the bush. We now have restrooms, both public and private for the process. (where is this going?, you are probably asking by now).

As most of you know that would be reading this, my wife is in a wheelchair. She is in it because she cannot walk any longer. She can stand for short periods but does not have the balance to walk or maneuver well. Most if not all bathroom functions require mobility. To get down to basics, my wife requires assistance for her bathroom functions. (she would probably not approve of this post - but hey, it is what it is) That is the point of this post.

Try taking a wheelchair bound person of the opposite gender to a bathroom when travelling. As I said above - "bathrooming" is a pretty basic need. My wife will signal a need for a stop and then we spend exit after exit, or rest stop after rest stop trying to find a family restroom (single party, oversized, unisex, handicapped equipped restroom becoming available slowly around the world) or a single setup with a lockable door that we can both fit into. We start looking and usually take hours finding a suitable place. It is extraordinarily frustrating to me and her - as well as being a physical challenge for her. I have the utmost respect for those that are installing the family restrooms. They are heaven sent. I just wish every rest stop would have one.

So, next time you are travelling and have the need to use the facilities; when you are able to stop, walk in, do your business, and leave in one stop - be grateful your 401K is all that has taken a hit. Hey, at least you've got your health, and an empty bladder.

I do highly recommend travelling to the limits of your health, finances, and desires; even if it is a bit difficult. The rewards are many. And, if the time comes where you are unable to travel you will have the memories.

CHAPTER EIGHT

REALIZATION

This is one of the posts that I have gotten a lot of comments on. People sharing that despair, people applauding the attempt at capturing the moment, and people offering blessings and kind thoughts. Thanks to all for the show of support.

Monday, February 15, 2010

And then we wept... - originally posted 3-17-09

I am not really sure what this post is to accomplish. It is a bit of a catharsis for me. I hope it will be informational for some, possibly even inspirational for others that may be going through a similar event in their life (although I profoundly hope there would be no others going through what we are - I know there are)

Sunday as we were getting ready to leave Florida for home, my wife started weeping rather uncontrollably. Being the tough macho guy that I am, I kept a stiff upper lip - for about 30 seconds. I HATE seeing my wife cry (or any other loved one), especially a sad, wailing, cry. I asked her what was wrong, but it was one of the teary events where you cannot even talk. She was brushing her teeth at the time, and between the toothpaste, toothbrush, and weeping - communication was not possible. So, I just was just there. Then I teared up myself. Watching her, a grown woman, RN, mother of six, and grandmother of two (with another on the way) not being able to really brush her teeth (we have an electric brush for home but travel with a normal one) struck me as one of the saddest things I have ever seen. Her coordination to really do the "brushing" motion is just not there anymore. So, we wept together. She for, at the time, an unknown reason; me, for what she was going through and what we have to face going forward.

As we got in the car later, she broke down again saying goodbye to her mother. I had a hard time with this one as well as I knew she was unfathomably sad. Goodbyes are always hard. As we got on the road, we composed ourselves a bit. Then we talked. Now, I don't know how many of you have or have had a loved one on death row. (actually, not a great comparison as there is always a chance of the governor calling - pretty sure this is above the governor's pay grade) Talk about an elephant in the room! We have talked in small circles around it, but never really in depth or details. This was pretty much the same except she started it with a tearful look and a question that ripped at my heart. She asked me through sobs "Will this be the last time I see my mother's house? Will I die before we get back?" By now, she was crying uncontrollably, and I was having trouble seeing the road. I had no witty response. I had no great comeback. I just told her - "We will make a point to.".

I don't remember exactly what was said next, or how we got there; but I told her I was very, very sorry she was sick. I told her I would give almost anything if she was not. We were now weeping again (being a tough, macho type - maybe I was just tearing up a bit - weeping sounds a bit wimpy). She told me she was sorry I had to deal with her. I told her I was where I should be. If I did not want to be where I was, I would leave. I reminded her I was in for the duration.

We rode in silence for a while. I am not sure about her, but I still found my eyes getting wet from time to time. There was once about two hours later where she had dozed off. I looked over at this woman that I married over 35 years ago. She was shaking with her Parkinson's tremors with her hands curled on her lap. She looked so helpless....and sick, I guess. I remembered how just three years ago we were saying goodbye as she headed for work. Her loss of her physical self has been amazingly rapid. I found myself reaching for a napkin to dry my eyes. Luckily, she has not lost any of her mental self. She is still crazy, funny, and enjoys a laugh. We just have to work harder to find things to laugh about.

We made it through the rest of the ride with the elephant safely in the back seat. No more discussions, no more tears. We even laughed a bit from time to time.

One of the things that Carol and I did not ever really do was address the elephant in the room that was her impending demise. We talked around it, and beside it, and everywhere else except directly about it. There were times immediately after her death that I wished we had.

Some of the decisions that I had to make could have been made a bit easier had we discussed it. Now that sounds selfish, and maybe it is, but I am making the point to advise any of you that are facing something similar to talk about any wishes, desires, or thoughts you may have about the end of life. We do not speak much of death. Even though, as I pointed out above, it is one of the few things we humans all share; we do not discuss it. I am guilty as well, by the way.

CHAPTER NINE

CURRENT

Up to now all the posts in the blog Livingwithasnowman.blogspot.com have been excerpts and reprints from my original blog www.JustSomePosts.blogspot.com. This marks the time and post where I became current. All the previous posts were done on the original blog as I wrote them, but as you can see from the dates at the top of each, they were reprints. From here out, any posts that were concerning Carol and her disease were solely posted on the www.livingwithasnowman.blogspot.com blog.

Saturday, February 20, 2010
We are up to date
OK, that gets us current. If you are starting here PLEASE go to the first post and read at least the first one. I advise reading them all as they are part of the documentation of the progression of the disease and our mindset from then to now.

From here on I will try to post thoughts and updates with some regularity.

Comments and suggestions are welcomed.

Welcome aboard!

I was not sure where I was going to go with the blog from this point. I wrote (and still write) from emotion. I was sure there were going to be many, many more days and events that would evoke strong emotions, but I both Carol and I were approaching more of an acceptance of what was and what would be. I think you can see a difference in the tome from here forward. You can see I had the same thoughts back eight years ago as well!

What next?

I know I have not posted anything new since the recap of all the existing posts from my original blog. This is turning out to be more difficult than I thought. If you read the previous posts you may have noted a theme - I was typically writing from emotion or passion from the moment. To try to post "informationally" is harder than I imagined when I thought of doing this separate blog. I am still working on how to get motivated to write without it becoming just a medical chart of my wife's disease.

A quick update on that - we continue to battle the daily battles; dressing, eating, using the facilities, etc. All seem to be more difficult as days go by. We have been playing with the medications to try to work on what my wife sees as her most annoying symptom - the tremors. It amazes me how such a small change can in dosage can affect her so much. She is now taking 1 1/2 tablets of 25/100 Sinemet (carbidopa/levadopa) every three hours. We have tried going to two tablets every three hours. That one half of a tablet - 33% more totally sedates her. My daughter (that helps care for her during the day when I am at work) and I both have been amazed at how "drugged" that small increase makes her. We also tried 1 tablet every two hours, but that seems not to work as well. So we stay at 1 1/2.

I will continue to work on trying to formulate a format for this so I can do posts regularly. Like I said, I don't want it to turn into a medical chart; but I also realize I can't wait for a passionate moment to do a post like I did in the past. Any ideas or suggestions are welcomed.

If you know anyone with this disease, or you yourself have been diagnosed with MSA - my wife and I would love to hear from you. Drop me a response and we will get back to you. From what I read there are about 7 people per million that have this evil disease. That means there are not a whole lot of people, but there are enough that communication and fellowship is possible.

CHAPTER TEN

OUT OF SEQUENCE

At the outset I told you I would try to retain the original "flavor" and tone of the blog, even when it involves mistakes. This is a post that I did out of sequence as I missed it when extracting the posts from the original blog. Chronologically it belongs up a bit, but this is where I posted it originally.

Sunday, March 21, 2010

Excuse me, are you a rock star? Originally posted April 22,2009

Sorry, I just found this one from the past that I apparently forgot to post when I was "catching up". I was getting ready to post some thoughts on Torticollis and remembered this.

Spasmodic Torticollis. Great name for a rock band, yes? Cervical Dystonia. Also a good one. Both sound like a lead-in for a heavy metal band with big hair. Well, we have entered the rock band era with my wife's disease. And now, the coliseum is proud to present....................
.......Cervical Dystonia!!!

These two heavy metal names are both monikers of a disease of which my wife now is suffering. As a side effect of her primary illness, we get to sample an entire array of diseases – as symptoms of multiple system atrophy.

Cervical Dystonia is (in layman's terms – I am just now learning about this, over the last few hours) where the muscles of the neck spasm and/or contract on their own. It is annoying and according to my wife (and common sense) very uncomfortable to painful. When she gets tired, excited, or emotional more than a bit, her neck pulls her head towards her chest. This is actually called anterocollis when it happens this way. There are other names for pulling to the side or to the back. I am not sure how common this is, but in her case she cannot pick her head up on her own. I have to push/pull her head to the correct position and hold it there while things calm down.

Ain't life grand! Rock on, dude!!

One of the especially frustrating things about MSA is that it can and does cause many, many other issues. Due to the blog posts and being active in MSA groups online, I have gotten a lot of questions that start with "My wife/husband/sister/brother/lover/patient/I have or has xxxxxxx (where xx...xx is a symptom). Could this be caused by MSA?" The answer is "YES" in most cases. Since MSA is a brain disease and the brain controls all, almost any symptom can be caused by MSA, directly or indirectly. The "good news" if you can call it that, it that at least a lot of these symptoms can be treated. MSA defies direct treatment, but some of the symptoms and accompanying diseases/afflictions can be treated. To have something that medical personnel CAN treat is a blessing. Then, there are some that cannot be treated easily or effectively either like cervical dystonia.

CHAPTER ELEVEN

This post addresses exactly what I was talking about previously; there is no treatment, remission, or cure for MSA (and a lot of the other alphabet diseases). This makes each doctor visit an exercise in futility for the most part. The visits are necessary as we do need prescriptions written, therapy ordered, and just a general check of bodily functions; but it is very frustrating to walk in and be reminded there is nothing to be done to check the progress of the disease in any serious way.

Sunday, April 11, 2010

To be, or not... (addtional apologies to the Bard)

One of the things we have come to expect out of medical providers and the field of medicine in this the modern world, is the ability to provide a cure and/or treatment for disease and sickness. I know I have addressed this issue before, but I am at it again as I find the lack of treatment the most frustrating part of my wife's illness from my point of view. The inability to do ANYTHING is unbelievably hard to deal with. Going to a doctor that specializes in parkinsonism and/or MSA is still going to get you an exam, a re-evaluation of medication from a helping with symptoms perspective, and then a pat on the back with a "see you in six months". Knowing that even if she had cancer we could be doing something, is almost too much to bear. (I am in no way making light of cancer. I realize cancer in its many forms is still one of the largest killers of people. BUT, I am making the point that all but the smallest of percentages of cancer have some chemo, radiation, or surgical procedure that can be done to at least improve the chances of survival and/or cause a remission.)

Dealing with the incessant decline of her ability to do what we all take for granted is frustrating for all of us, especially my wife. We now have to basically feed her with every meal unless it is a simple finger food. Going to the bathroom and all that encompasses is a challenge that grows with every day. Picking up her cup from her chair side for a drink is becoming a challenge for her. We have no relief from the inexorable march of this disease. Just this morning my wife looked up at me with tears in her eyes and said, "I don't want to be sick any more". I told her I would give most anything if she was not.

I have commented before that to live with someone that is on death row, so to speak, is a sobering experience. As much as I try, I cannot fathom what she is going through. Yesterday morning I was putting away in her closet some of her winter clothes while she watched. I came out of the closet and she was crying. I went to her and asked why. She sobbed to me "Will I ever wear those again?" I just hugged her. Unless you are faced with something like she is, you would not even think that way.

I know a lot of people out there, maybe even some of the ones that might read this post, have friends, family, or even themselves, that have been saved from a horrible death by modern medicine. I know there are people now that are going through the horrors of chemo and/or radiation; or facing an amputation or transplant. However, as horrible as those things are...

Be glad you do not have one of the alphabet diseases where NOTHING can be done.

I did get a few negative comments on this one due to the fact that it was perceived that I was making light of people with cancer or other diseases. I was and am definitely, not! Cancer has taken many, many members of my family. I know it kills untold thousands of people annually. I was just saying that at least the oncologist can say "let's discuss your options for treatment" in most cases. With MSA and other alphabet diseases it is just, "see you at the next visit" with the implied (if you are still able). I do wish everyone with any disease or illness all the best. To have any serious disease is a horrible thing.

CHAPTER TWELVE

COMMUNICATION

You can see by the dates that I had slowed down in my posts. The day to day grind of the disease and life had taken over. Some acceptance had occurred (with both Carol and myself) and we had just settled in for the ride. I was getting many comments and emails from people reading the blog (and still get some today after all these years!) and felt somewhat obligated to continue posting.

Communicating with Carol was becoming more and more difficult as her disease progressed. She went from not being able to speak clearly enough to hold telephone conversation to not being able to type on a keyboard. She was slowly being cut off from normal conversations.

Sunday, May 23, 2010
What did you say?

I know I have not posted for a while. As I said previously, without making this just a daily or weekly report of the disease, I just cannot be motivated to write. Most of the posts prior were "of the moment" type. I am still wrestling with this. Here are some thoughts today however.

Most, if not all of you reading this can turn to someone else in the room and make a comment on it. If you want to send me your thoughts on this post, you can type a comment. When your phone rings, you answer it and have a conversation if it is someone you want to talk to. Now, imagine none of that were possible.

That is where my wife is now. I tell her that her world is slowly getting smaller. It started by her not being able to drive where she wanted. Then it became so she could not walk where she wanted. That restricts her physically. Slowly, her ability to talk is being taken away. I have said "excuse me", "what did you say", or just "huh" 8,468 times in the past month. I know it annoys both of us.

What does it mean when you can't speak? You can't let people know what you are thinking. There are schools of thought that

profess speech as one of the defining features of our humanity. She can make known what she needs, and most of her wants; but the act of discussing what she feels or being able to hold a conversation is gone. Like I said, she lives in a little world. People don't call her because they cannot understand her on the phone. People don't talk to her because they cannot understand her responses. When we go to the doctor now, they end up speaking to me because I am usually translating after the first few words anyway.

So, modern technology has given us many other ways of communicating - right? Texting, IM-ing, email, blogging, etc. That has helped some, and still is a bit. But, try doing any of those things when your tremors are so bad that you cannot hit the keys. It can take her two to three minutes to type a text with one sentence - and then it will be mostly misspelled words. Emails are OK, but for her to answer one can take all evening and would fail a second grade writing class.

I can only experience this through her frustration. I feel so bad for her. I have tried to think of anything that might help, but I am at a loss. I see her world slowly (or actually, too damn quickly) closing in around her. Not being able to communicate with family and friends is horrible for her. We continue to do what we can. She continues to do less and less.

CHAPTER THIRTEEN

MELTING

I knew from experience that one of the big issues with MSA was (and still is to a great extent) the lack of knowledge and information out there. We were facing symptoms and issues that we had no idea of how to handle. As I met other patients and caregivers online I found there were a lot of similarities in the issues and symptoms all were facing. They may vary in severity and are definitely varied in the timeframe in which they occur, but most patients were experiencing the same things Carol was facing, and that my daughter and myself were in trying to deal with them. You can see a turn in the blog posts at this point as I try to become more informative. I felt (and still feel) if something we learned to make life more manageable or better for the patient or caregiver could be shared it could help others. I obviously was still dealing with the MSA demon myself however, as was Carol.

Tuesday, July 6, 2010
Just looking for some shade
I know I have not posted in over six weeks. I mentioned a while back that this was harder than I imagined when I started. In some ways it is probably different than you may imagine. It is not that I have nothing to say. In most cases it is that I have too much to say. But out of commitment to the four people and a frog that read this, I thought I would write something.

The title of this blog was one of those things that came from passion of the moment. My wife was having a particularly bad couple of days and I told her "you are like a snowman - melting right in front of my eyes." Later that month was when I started this blog. Did you ever try to save snow? I have never seen it done. Just the act of touching it, changes it. You can put a container of snow into your freezer and when you go to get it out it is ice. If you don't put it in the freezer, it is water - in a very short time. My wife is a bit different. She is still her. As I have said before, we still joke and laugh - we just have to work a bit harder at it, and we may stop a bit sooner. She is still the wonderful person I fell in love with almost forty years ago. Her physical self is changing. This damned disease is wreaking havoc on her ability to do most anything. It is like the snowman in the sun. It may be below freezing, but if the sun hits the snowman - it melts a bit. It changes. There is not much you can do about it.

I have mentioned the other "joys" of this disease. MSA is a beast. It not only causes problems on its own; due to the fact it affects the brain it calls in a lot of other "helpers" to add to the challenges. I know I have written about the spinal torticollis (cervical dystonia) that my wife has to deal with. This is a fun disease all on its own. When partnered up with MSA, it is a real joy. We are constantly picking my wife's head up now. She is constantly leaning forward. It makes almost any activity a real challenge.

For over the past month my wife has had to deal with another alphabet disease - TMJ. Temporomandibular joint (TMJ) is actually the name of the jaw joint. However, it had become synonymous with the disorder of the joint that causes pain and discomfort when opening or closing the jaw - chewing for example. This pain has been so bad that she has not eaten solid food for over six weeks, except to experiment to see if it is better (which it has not been). We are slowly becoming experts on the world of liquid nourishment. Bless the Ensure, Boost, protein powder, V8 Splash, Mott's manufacturers. I have also become quite proficient at making a protein shake that can be ingested without gagging.

Again, I compare this disease to the melting of a snowman. The advance of the disease is relentless. The complications are trying. The challenges to everyday living are monumental. What we both would not give for just one day of "normal" - old normal. Like it was five years ago before this disease started dominating our lives. Although the end of that one day would be hell for both of us. In fact, knowing how the day would end would probably make it hell itself.

Oh well, we will just keep looking for shade.

Again I mention - if you or a loved one is dealing with this disease; we would love to hear from you. One of the other characteristics of this disease versus most others is you almost never meet anyone else with it. There just are not enough people afflicted (thankfully) to form much of a community. That makes the disease worse in that you are facing it alone and without

information or much support. Please contact us by posting here.
or emailing me - gumbypoole@aol.com

The complications and accompanying diseases and symptoms of MSA make it particularly challenging for the patient, family, and any caregivers. The progression is relentless, and the physical impairments are many. Torticollis and TMJ are just two of the auxiliary diseases that Carol had to deal with. This made each day an "adventure" where we knew not what was coming. Carol's ability to deal with the disease, the impairments, and the pain still astound me today. As I have stated before, her ability to handle this adversity with such grace and stoic demeanor are a testament to her as a person.

CHAPTER FOURTEEN

LIFE GOES ON

I remember the event that prompted this post like it was yesterday. When my daughter called me (see below for details) it shook me to my core. The fact that I was a minimum of five hours away from them made it worse. This is about the guilt that a caregiver can (and probably will) have on not "being there" every minute of every day and acting as an impenetrable shell against all things bad and painful — an unachievable goal by any estimation. Without further ado:

Tuesday, August 10, 2010

Continuing Saga

My job requires some overnight travel. I am lucky to have a boss that is very understanding of our familial condition and my requirement to be at home as much as possible. However, I still have to go away at times. This past weekend was one of these. My wife and I are also lucky to have six children. Our oldest daughter is acting as my wife's primary caregiver currently, when I am at work or away. I am still very mindful of the fact that my wife is more comfortable and secure when I am there, but realize we are very fortunate to have the help we do.

I left last Thursday and returned last evening (Monday). I got a call from my daughter yesterday prior to my leaving to come home. I could tell by the hesitant way she started the conversation, she was not looking forward to saying what she had to say. This has happened a few times before. My mind always starts racing from here to there thinking of the possibilities (which truly are endless) of what she could have happened. She has called to tell me my youngest daughter had wrecked my car, that my wife had this problem or that, or other such news. This occasion was about my wife. It seems she had fallen. It was during a bathroom maneuver. Somehow the wheelchair moved out from under them and my wife and daughter ended up on the floor. So far, not too bad. It also seems that my wife's hand ended up under my daughter - still not too bad. Now the bad part. The pinkie finger on my wife's hand had curled up and bent in a fashion that caused my daughter to crush the finger.

They told me later that in the moment after the fall, while "taking inventory" of what had happened, my wife cried out "my hand!" My daughter realized it was under her and pulled it out. The nail from the pinkie finger remained behind on the floor. The finger was bent in a weird fashion and appeared broken (X-rays later confirmed this). Blood was everywhere due to the torn off fingernail. It apparently was a quite gruesome sight, and as you might imagine - a quite painful one as well. Getting a nail ripped off of a finger and breaking the final joint is not a pleasant experience, I would imagine (I have had a nail ripped off, and a broken hand - but never at the same time).

I came home last night and was shown the hand. It looks like it has been beaten with a hammer. It is very swollen, and extremely black and blue. I did not examine the finger yet, it was dressed and had been bleeding, so we felt it was better to just leave it alone. I will see it this morning when I re-dress it.

My point of this, other than reporting? There is now lots of guilt to go around. My daughter's guilt at not preventing the fall. Her guilt at landing on the finger, etc. Then there is my guilt. If I had been home there would likely not have been a fall. The problem here is one of reality. We all have lives to live. I would love to stay at home and take care of my wife and be with her all the time. Financial obligations do not allow that to even be considered. My daughter's guilt is understandable. However, accidents happen. The goal is to make them as infrequent as possible, and if they do occur - as benign as possible. My wife and I are very lucky to have her to help as she does.

If you are faced with a loved one that has this, or another debilitating disease; you too are (or will be) faced with the question of "do I go to work or do I stay?" Unless your financial circumstances are such that you can live without the income, the answer will be "No". If you are a caregiver, you will always worry about every bump and bruise (as you should). You cannot let fear paralyze your actions. In trying to prevent any danger or injury, you are probably opening up the opportunity for more. Life and living are a risk. Pain and suffering are a part of life. This damn disease should be pain and suffering enough for a family for a lifetime.

The saga continues, life goes on - such as it is.

The physical wounds healed. The psychological ones, not so much. My daughter, my wife, and myself fought against these demons until her death and beyond. The desire and sometimes the need to be a superhero when caring for someone is great. (this applies to moms as well, in my estimation – shout out to all the moms out there!) You want to prevent anything bad from happening, and that includes being put on the street due to lack of payment for a place to live. That means you cannot be there every hour of every day. Then there is the fact that even if you were, you could not prevent the bad things from happening. I would hope that those of you that are caring for another can permit yourself to be human. May any and all of your injuries – physical and mental – be minor.

CHAPTER FIFTEEN

I KNOW YOU'RE IN THERE

This is another lament about the way that MSA and some other alphabet diseases take away the ability to communicate. I mentioned this earlier. This was one of Carol's most frustrating symptoms. To watch her be closed off from the world was very hard for all of us. For her to be closed off from the world was hell for her.

Tuesday, August 31, 2010

HELLO...?

I have mentioned before that communication for my wife (and those of us trying to communicate with her) is a very, VERY frustrating thing. I am travelling again this week and one of the things I always try to do is call her at least once a day just to "check in". This is so frustrating for her and me. She has trouble holding the phone to her mouth/ear, and that combined with her inability to speak clearly and with volume makes a phone call a frustrating experience. She actually does not get many phone calls now from anyone but myself just for that reason. I know she likes to hear from me (and others) so I make a point to call.

It always makes me so sad to hear her; actually, to not be able to hear her. I am constantly saying "I did not hear that" or just "what" or "excuse me"; at almost every comment. I end up cutting the call short just because of the frustration level for her and myself. What is the saddest to me however, is when I call her and she does not answer. What I get (or now got, because Verizon changed our voicemail service and her message was erased) is her voice from three or so years ago. It would tear me up to hear her bright, cheerful, clear voice with volume telling me she was not available. As I have commented before, it is amazing how quickly this disease takes away that which those of us that are not afflicted take for granted; like eating, speaking, walking, driving, etc. It always amazed me that her voice could change so much in such a short time.

We always get some form of conversation in, however; and she made my day today when I said "I did not have anything particular to tell you. I just wanted to say hi". Her response was "I am glad you did".

Like I said, we are just searching for the shade.

This is one of the symptoms that we never were able to mitigate. In Carol's case her voice went (no phone, no conversation), the motor skills to operate her fingers went (no keyboard), and even her eye movement was compromised by another disease that came along for the ride with the MSA – nystagmus (no reading). I was (and am) the introvert of our family. Carol was the social one, with contacts everywhere we went. As she lost her ability to communicate she intentionally cut herself off from friends and somewhat from family to save the embarrassment (more for the other person than herself) and difficulty of trying to hold a conversation of any type. We did talk about how small her world was getting. She (and I) hated it!

CHAPTER SIXTEEN

JUST SETTLING IN FOR THE RIDE

I would like to tell you that I was awesome every moment of every day; taking care of Carol's every need, answering every call with a smile and always having a bounce in my step. But, as you probably already figured out, I was (and am) not! I struggled as well. I still tell people to this day that MSA and other alphabet diseases affect the whole family. Now, when I got too wrapped up in self-pity I came back down to earth as I looked at my wife and helped her with some simple task that even a toddler does for themselves. This is after one of these events and the self-reflection that occurred.

Wednesday, September 22, 2010
Update
I was working on a catchy title for this one, but the muse is not with me.

This is just an update. I feel somewhat obligated to write occasionally and was not feeling particularly motivated about any one subject.

Like most humans, I find myself feeling sorry for me sometimes. If I can't do or get what I want for some reason, I lament - if only to myself. There are a lot of tasks that I do now that I never did before. I have always had no problem with domestic chores. I enjoy cooking (not talking about grilling a steak or hamburger, but making a meal), I have done the laundry for over a decade as one of my household duties, and many other things. Since my wife has been incapacitated by her disease, I have to do a lot of "stuff" or it does not get done. We are lucky in a sense that our daughter that helps with her Mom during the day is a bit of a neat freak. I have never been one for gratuitous cleaning, she is helping a lot with the actual cleaning vs the wiping the middle of the counters that I do. However, that still leaves a lot of other things that must be done. So, for the most part I get them done.

When I notice me feeling sorry for myself, I just think of my wife.

There have been times that I or someone would comment something like "I really don't want to go to the store" or "Man, I hate having to pick her up now, it is so inconvenient" or whatever. On a few of those occasions I have been snapped back to reality by a quiet comment from my wife saying "I wish I could". When you cannot go or do anything, you gain appreciation for everything. As I will complain about having to go to the grocery store, she admits she would love to go. As I whine about making another meal, she mentions that it would be wonderful to cook again. And so it goes.

Imagine you sitting in a chair. Sitting, sitting, sitting.... That is your life. Having a conversation with someone is out, because they cannot hear or understand you. You can't use the phone, because you can't dial the numbers - and if someone dials them for you, the person on the other end can't hear you anyway. You can watch TV, but you can't change the channel because you can't work the remote. The computer is a wonderful device to communicate and keep up with friends and family, right? What if you can't work the keys anymore? How about a book? Can't hold it still and the eyes wander so much and blur so often; not really practical.

So, can't walk, drive, talk, type, read, and so on and so on. At least you can sit in comfort, right? Not really anymore. The tremors are there most of the time to irritate and aggravate. The torticollis continually pulls your head to your chest and bends you forward. Your hands and arms cramp as they draw up and curl inward. Your rear end hurts from sitting so much. You get the idea.

So, when I don't feel like going and getting my wife out of bed, or making another meal, or doing a load of laundry; I just think how it would be to not be able to do anything. I don't feel sorry for myself anymore. The shade is getting harder to find.

If you know someone that is caring for a loved one that is ill, remember them. Give them a call. Give them a break. I respectfully honor and offer thanks and good thoughts for any of you out there doing so. Enjoy what you can, when you can. Appreciate what you do have. Don't regret what you don't.

The alphabet diseases are a horrible physical burden, but I think the psychological burden was and is sometimes greater. The patient is left totally aware and alert mentally, they just cannot perform the physical side of what they may want or need to do. Being totally dependent on another is somewhat a loss of self. Knowing that it is very likely to not get any better and in fact will get worse, is debilitating to the patient and if not careful also to the caregiver. This can lead to a place where all just give up. I know I came close to that point many times. Carol did as well. But, we did try to do what we could when we could and always, always tried to laugh – at life and ourselves.

CHAPTER SEVENTEEN

SOMETHING TO LOOK FORWARD TO

Multiple System Atrophy has no cure, no true remission, and is 100% fatal. Being given a death sentence changes your outlook on life. I know it did for Carol and for me. The trivial things do not seem as important. The idiot that cuts you off in traffic is just a minor annoyance, soon to be forgotten. Carol and I did our best to enjoy what we could when we could (yes, this phrase is a common thread and one I use to this day). We did that with travel in a large part.

Wednesday, October 27, 2010
Me and the elephant again
Every time I look, it has been over a month since I posted here. For my fan (I know you are out there), I am sorry. As I have said previously, it is hard to get motivated to do this. Emotion and passion drove the beginning and most of the earlier posts.

The melting continues. MSA is a cruel, dastardly illness. It is evil in the way it affects EVERYTHING! I feel so bad for my wife as she is dealing with being able to do less and less. Her speech, posture, grip, facial expressions, vision, movement, and overall comfort are affected in ways you cannot imagine if you are not going through it. To deal with it second hand is bad, to be the person afflicted has to be hell on earth.

One of the ways we have dealt with this disease has been to try to have something in the not too distant future to look forward to. When my wife was first diagnosed, we made a deal to go on a cruise. We did late that year. We have since been on another cruise; and are leaving on yet another in a week and a half. By the way, if you are the caregiver of someone with a similar affliction, I can recommend cruising as a good vacation. Every modern cruise ship I have looked at has handicapped accessible rooms, family-style restrooms, and are generally workable for a wheelchair bound person. With the meals, entertainment, and travel happening all around you, limited mobility is not as big an issue. The pricing is very competitive with a stay at a decent hotel. This is especially true when you factor in that the food and entertainment are included for the most part. I also recommend NCL. The "freestyle" cruising is the way to go. Our last three cruises have been on NCL and it is the only way to go. (OK, NCL - a free or discounted cruise for my wife would be welcomed)

I am looking upon this trip with some sadness however. Although we are both looking forward to it, we both realize that this could very well be our last "big" trip. My wife's condition is making it tougher to do the daily things that have to be done, especially when in new and different surroundings. Now, we have not discussed this. I have mentioned the "elephant in the room" problem that occurs (at least for us) when acknowledging this disease. Unless you have been in the situation of having a loved one diagnosed with a progressive and fatal illness, you probably cannot imagine how discussing it is avoided. I just know that we are having more and more problems dealing with day to day activities here to realize that future trips like this probably will not be possible. I know my wife understands this as well.

Facing this realization, among all the others, is one of the things that makes this disease so damn evil. My wife and I have been married for 37+ years. We have raised six kids to adulthood. We did without a lot of things over the years, especially for us. We had a reasonable existence and tried to give our kids a life they would and could look back fondly on. We finally got to a point that we could have enjoyed life with each other when MSA came in. Again, we have not discussed this a lot. This is not just an elephant in the room, but an entire menagerie - rhino in the room, lion in the room, etc. As I have said before here, we still enjoy what we can, when we can. We still laugh as much as possible, just maybe not as long or as loudly.

Anyway, think of us on the ship in the blue waters of the Caribbean sea in early November. The snow is melting anyway, we might as well go to the tropics.

As it turned out, this was our last big trip. We took the cruise in December of 2010 and Carol died the end of May 2011. We enjoyed it, but I will admit it was hard on me. I hope Carol enjoyed it. My youngest daughter went with us and we tried to do what Carol wanted to do within our physical limitations.

I mention above that I think cruising is a great activity for a person with limited mobility. I still feel that way. I will add, look at the ports. In a lot of them the ships use tenders to get from ship to shore. You will not be able to negotiate the transfer to and from a tender on most ships and in most ports, in my experience. If you want to get off the ship with a person in a wheelchair, make sure you are going to ports where the ship will pull to a dock. In almost every case getting on and off the ship can be accommodated at a dock versus with a tender (a smaller boat) at ports without docks. Also remember that you are in foreign countries in most cases. The USA has the American with Disabilities Act (ADA). The ADA assures that when in the USA you can expect wheelchair access to almost anything along with other accommodations geared towards those with reduced mobility. That is NOT the case in most of the foreign ports, at least in the Caribbean. Now, we enjoyed the relaxed and uncrowded atmosphere on the boat when most everyone was on shore. However, if you are looking at a land excursion or other reasons for leaving the boat, some research is definitely in order. I still recommend cruising, but let the buyer beware.

CHAPTER EIGHTEEN

LOSING STEAM

At this point a lot of the emotion had gone out of me. I was getting hundreds of hits to the site monthly along with many emails from family and patients afflicted with MSA and other alphabet diseases. For this reason, I felt I had to "stay in touch", even though I was not so motivated to do so. This was what came of that. This was a couple of weeks back from the cruise with my daughter. We were all drained and as much as we were avoiding it (the elephant!) we were all down a bit realizing that this cruise had been our last. We were not thinking about impending death or anything that morbid, just the fact that the trip had taken too much out of us.

Monday, December 27, 2010

Hello

I realize it has been a LONG time since a new post. I just am having trouble coming up with original posts. I do not want to do a litany of problems or complaints and I have not been moved with any specific ideas. I have a lot to write, but it would be a rehash of previous post.

If you have not read all the posts here, please do so.

Please, if you have an idea for a post, or a question...recommend or ask!

A real post will follow soon, promise.

Since the above was such a short post and the next one is almost a continuation of it, here it is:

Wednesday, January 12, 2011

This is where we're at

I promised an update and a "real" post in my last abbreviated one. So, even though I still am not sure what to write - here we go.

The disease continues its advance. My wife is at a point now where swallowing is a problem at times. We sometimes work for 10 minutes on one pill. The good news is she does not have to take much. We have cut out the vitamins and supplements, it became too much of a hassle every day to get them down. Also, between her jaw problems (TMJ, see previous posts) and the swallowing, we have to be aware of her nutrition. Especially without her supplements and vitamins. Thank heavens for Boost.

Speaking is pretty much gone now. She will croak out something from time to time, but mostly she talks in a whisper. With my poor hearing that means a LOT of repeating and questioning. I feel like we are playing 20 questions a lot of the time. We do have a speech therapy session scheduled for next week. I am not sure what can be done at this point, but we will try. It has to be frustrating to her to not be able to communicate. I know it is for me on this end. We do have an eye blink system set up for yes and no questions. I felt like that was "giving up" at first, but it definitely helps. I decided some communication was better than none.

Her life pretty much revolves around her recliner and the TV. Her eyes and concentration do not allow her to read. (she had trouble focusing her eyes and they have a tendency to dart around - another wonderful part of this disease) Her tremors and lack of ability to move make using a computer out of her reach as well. Throw in the above problems with speech and that leaves TV watching as her pastime. The lack of speech even makes using her phone an impossibility.

I really had no plan today, so I guess that is it. I thought I would at least update things. I would still like some responses from any and all that read this out there. I see by my statistics and such that there are some of you from all points in the northern hemisphere. Drop me an email. If you are going through this disease as a patient or a caregiver, I would love to hear from you. If you have questions, ask. We'll be here.

I guess you can sense the frustration here. I definitely feel it come back as I read this. The helplessness that one feels when there is nothing to be done for someone you love is a horrible thing. I felt so bad for Carol and how small her life had become, but she just pushed on.

As for the contact, I was getting many emails and some comments on the blog. I "met" some folks through this that I still keep up with today. They are now caregiver survivors also. We all just carry on as best we can.

CHAPTER NINETEEN

SUSTENANCE

As an RN Carol knew something of the disease she was afflicted with. Not a lot; as I have noted, we had to "train" many a nurse, doctor, or other medical personnel on what MSA was/is. Some things she told me at the beginning were "no feeding tube" and "no extraordinary measures" if she ended up in the hospital unresponsive. She made me promise both of these things and I kept my word through the end. My kids were angry with me the last night in the hospital when I made sure the hospital knew Carol had a DNR. I was determined to follow her wishes.

The feeding tube issue reared its ugly head during a doctor visit on the day I wrote this post. Carol had a swallowing function test and was basically told a feeding tube was imminent. Neither of us commented to the doctor or technician that had made that forecast, we just went out to eat.

Thursday, January 27, 2011

To eat or not to eat, that is the question.

I have done blogs on my other "all purpose blog" (http://www.justsomeposts.blogspot.com/) about how we Americans are obsessed with food and eating. Imagine yourself being told you cannot eat any more solids, nor can you drink any more liquids. That is where we are now.

We have a new addition to our list of ailments - Dysphagia - aka inability to swallow (or problems swallowing). Since about the first of December, my wife has been dealing with more and more problems related to eating and swallowing. She was (and is) having a lot of problems with both liquids and solids. (for those of you following this damned disease or caring for someone afflicted - dysphagia is a very common and expected symptom - be forewarned) She has problems doing with her lips, mouth, tongue, and throat what we all take for granted pretty much from the first minutes of life. Using a straw has become a challenge, as she cannot get the muscles of her mouth to do what needs to be done to get it to "suction" the liquid. Drinking liquids directly from a cup is a problem because of lack of control of the liquid and the chance of choking. (another note for those following along - pneumonia is the greatest threat with this disease and is the leading cause of death) Aspiration of the liquid, especially anything other than water, is very dangerous due to the inability to cough. My wife has a pretty good reflex cough, but almost no ability to cough "on cue". Actually, liquids can be harder to swallow than solids because of the amount of "control" required to keep from choking. This was something I had to learn, as it was counter-intuitive to me. Most of us take drinking a liquid to be a given and very easy to do versus eating solid food.

Today we went to the hospital for a modified barium swallow test. My wife had one done almost a year ago and was told other than a bit of slowness with her swallowing, all was well. Today was an entirely different story. She did the test, which involves swallowing (and chewing where necessary) various thicknesses of liquids and semi-solids infused with radioactive barium while having an X-ray taken of the mouth and throat. When we got the results, we were both taken a bit aback. The lady that administered the test, and gave us the results, calmly told us that she recommended that my wife avoid eating solid foods or drinking liquids of normal consistency. She said we should get her nutrition and fluid from semi-liquids of honey consistency (which I have since learned through the internet is an "official" consistency of Dysphagia products). We were further instructed to get her medications converted to liquid form and then give them in a product like applesauce or any "honey-like" liquid. I have also learned that there are a LOT of dysphagia products out there. Meal replacements, thickeners, etc. in a myriad of flavors and consistencies. Thank goodness for that.

So, my wife, an American through and through was faced with a life of thickened fluids as food. No more Chinese food, no more fast food, no more fried chicken, etc. Purees and thickened fluids were prescribed. I am not sure of her immediate reaction, but I know mine was one of shock. We have both known this day would come, but it was still a blow. The trip home was solemn and sad. Food is such a part of who we are it was almost like the amputation or removal of a body part. We mourned a bit and will continue to do so; but this is another loss among many that this disease has caused. So, we did what Americans do - she ate KFC fried chicken, slaw, mashed potatoes & gravy, and a fried apple pie for dinner. We will face the rest later.

Carol basically went on a thick liquid diet from that KFC meal forward. I learned how to make many somewhat palatable liquid meals. We bought thickening agents and used a food processor a lot. I am sure that "eating" became quite the chore for her, but she was very gracious in at least pretending to be enjoying whatever I or my daughter made for her to eat.

The feeding tube issue is a very personal one. I am not passing judgement on anyone that elects to have one or anyone that does not. I do not know what I would do in that respect. I knew and know that what we did was truly what Carol wanted.

CHAPTER TWENTY

Although the blog has gotten tens of thousands of views, the viewing is not evenly spread through of all the posts. The most viewed is the opening one, then this one is always in the top two or three. I am not sure why this one is read that much more than some of the others.

Sunday, February 20, 2011

Normalicy is a fallacy

I have done many posts on either of my two blogs on perspective. One thing this disease (Multiple System Atrophy for those of you just joining and not reading from the beginning) does is redefine normal. Normal depends on your perspective. To a single, childless person a normal morning is entirely different from a person with a spouse and children. A dictionary definition of normal is:

nor·mal   /ˈnɔrməl/ [nawr-muhl]
-adjective
1. conforming to the standard or the common type; usual; not abnormal; regular; natural.

This disease changes normal. This disease changes the definition of a good day. This disease changes everything. (I know a lot of diseases do, I can just comment from where I sit - no disrespect intended)

When I started this blog, it was for a couple of reasons. As you may know or have determined, all of the original posts on this blog are reprints from my other blog - Just Some Posts. I wanted to "clean up" the content there and give these posts their own space. I also was (and am) hoping for the addition of a specific audience. I was (and am) looking for people suffering from this disease or people caring for people afflicted with this disease. Although I would love to hear from any and all of you, when I say "looking for" I mean as an audience of readers. One of the real problems with this disease from our perspective is the isolation. You can see from the other blogs, Facebook pages, user groups, etc.; that this is the case worldwide. Medical personnel don't know what it is, the symptoms, or much else in a lot of cases. Caregivers and patients are begging for help in dealing with the symptoms and the trouble of getting a diagnosis (and not wanting one when it is this disease). We have yet to meet personally, a patient with the disease except at a convention/meeting in Nashville sponsored by the Shy-Drager Support Group (now the SDS/MSA Support Group - http://www.shy-drager.org/ - wonderful people and organization by the way), over two years ago. It is hard to find information, help, and/or relevant support for this disease and its symptoms. This is improving, but one thing that distresses me about these new support sites is they are so unconnected and disjointed. Everyone and every group is setting up their own sites. I guess I am doing the same here, so I can't be too critical.

My wife and I have been dealing with her symptoms and problems caused by this disease as they arise since 2006. As a problem/symptom would develop - lack of balance, inability to stand, severe tremors that made it impossible to hold silverware, slurring of speech, etc.; we have come up with solutions, or at least solutions that have helped us. We continually change our "normal". One real problem I have with these solutions is by the time we have them worked out, in a lot of cases, they are irrelevant. I tell my wife repeatedly that she is outrunning my fixes. For example, by the time we acquired proper weighted and sized silverware with non-slip plates with edges my wife had become unable to feed herself. Had we known that we would need them, and the products even existed, we would have been better for it. I had hoped this blog would alert some of you at earlier stages of the disease what to expect (at least from what happened to us - I do understand that this disease manifests itself in many different ways - there do however appear to be a lot of similarities) and how we dealt with it. I have tried to do some of this with these posts. I plan to do more with the next post, a complete listing of symptoms my wife has experienced and how we have dealt with it (when we had a "solution").

One other aspect of this disease is the pressure it puts on us with decisions. Small decisions, like what to eat or drink, when and where to go to the bathroom can have literal life and death implications. I don't want to sound overly dramatic, but it is true. One of my wife's real problems throughout this disease has been her syncope (fainting or "passing out"). We have used all the "tricks" and learned lots of our own to help with this, but she still passes out - some days a lot. The bathroom is our real nemesis. There are sometimes when she "goes away" for quite a time. We had an instance recently where she was "out" for 30 minutes and off and on for the better part of an hour in the bathroom. I did not have my cell phone and had no one to assist me or we would have called 911. I could not leave her and could not call. As I finally was able to get her into her wheelchair and out I asked her if she still wanted me to call 911. She was shocked as she did not remember the incident (normally the case) and did not want me to call (and was very glad I did not). As it turned out, we did not need emergency assistance. However, this could have been a life and death decision. Many other seemingly small decisions can be shown after the fact to have been near life and death. The stress involved with these decisions are part of the burden of this awful damned disease.

Like I promised above, my next post will be a recounting of my wife's major symptoms/problems and what we have done/did do to cope.

I am still looking for responses from people suffering from this disease or similar. Please comment or contact me.

As I said in the opening, this is one of the most read posts. I have gotten emails and contact from it as I requested as well. In fact I was contacted by a wife/caregiver not too long ago and she mentioned this and the following posts as her motivation.

Normal is an interesting concept. What is normal for some is very abnormal for another. We all want things to be "normal" but our "normal" might make another person or persons run screaming into the night! What became normal for Carol and myself was so far from the normal we had lived before as to be a different life. Change was the issue. Every day brought new challenges. But change became normal.

CHAPTER TWENTY-ONE

OFFERING ADVICE AND KNOWLEDGE

As I mentioned previously, I was always bothered by the fact that the disease was "outrunning us". A symptom would appear, and we would start working on something to overcome, mitigate, and/or help to make it livable. The issue was that the disease kept morphing into something different almost weekly. As you have seen if you have read to this point MSA has many, many difficult diseases that "tag along" with the main body of symptoms. This made it almost like we were fighting a different enemy each day. As we came up with solutions, the disease would move on and the solution would lose effectiveness. So, I thought it there had been some place for me to go to see how others coped with this symptom or that, we would have saved time. This is the first of three of the posts where I try to go into each symptom and share the things we found that helped Carol. I will do all three of these back-to-back.

Friday, March 25, 2011
Maybe this will help - Part 1
I had mentioned that I wanted to do a post outlining the problems my wife has experienced with Multiple System Atrophy and how we have worked to overcome them (where applicable). I am sitting here with her in a hospital room with lots of time so I thought that now would be good. I am doing this on my phone so forgive typing problems.

Realize MSA is a unique journey for each patient. The symptoms are similar (depending on the sub-type) but may occur earlier, later, or of a much greater or lesser degree of severity in almost all MSA patients. These symptoms, as well as the severity and timing are specific to my wife and her disease path. I hope there are enough similarities here to be of use to someone. This is NOT meant to be a medical dissertation. It will not be scientifically correct in all minutiae. As far as I know, it is all correct and based in fact, but I am not a medical professional, except in as much as a caregiver for any

MSA patient has to be. (OK, back on a computer with a real keyboard now)

My wife's disease manifested itself first as syncope (fainting). The things we learned about syncope and some of the "tricks" we have learned to deal with it are as follows:

Syncope or fainting is caused by a lack of oxygen to the brain. In MSA patients (as in most) this is usually caused by a drop in blood pressure. The brain cannot get enough blood to properly oxygenate, so to "save" itself it shuts down. This means the person containing the brain shuts down, thus fainting. When you faint you end up not standing any more, right? When you sit or lie down, your heart can get more blood to the brain because it is not fighting gravity any longer (or as much). Therefore, this is a defense mechanism the brain has for protection against lack of oxygen. Sensible, but dangerous and annoying to the person.

Going from cool (or even "normal" room temps) to hot (or even a bit warmer) causes the blood vessels near the skin to dilate (open up) to help cool the body. This means more blood goes to the skin (ever seen anyone flush when hot?). If more blood is in the skin area it cannot be in the brain. Hence, syncope. My wife's most annoying and sometimes dangerous episodes were when she would get out of her air-conditioned car upon arriving at work. When she was walking across the blacktop of the parking lot, (or just turning off the car and opening the door) she would pass out. This happened a few times, to the point the hospital where she worked thought she had a drug or alcohol problem. We started being very careful about temperature changes, especially from cool to hot. We would turn off the A/C in the car prior to arriving at our destination. We would allow some time with the door open, just sitting, waiting for the body to adjust to the temperature.

Syncope also occurs, especially among MSA patients upon positional changes. From a prone position to a sitting position can cause dizziness and fainting. The big one is from a prone or sitting to a standing. This is called orthostatic hypotension and is one of the defining features of MSA. To help this, try to avoid sudden changes in position (going up). Clenching the muscles of the legs and buttocks can help in forcing blood out of the lower part of the body (or to prevent it from entering as fast) and staying available for the brain.

When standing, it is harder for the heart to pump blood to the brain. A certain "extra" amount of blood goes to the lower part of the body. In a person with a fully functioning sympathetic nervous system, this is not a problem. The heart rate is increased pumping the blood at an increased rate (raising blood pressure) briefly to counteract this. In a MSA patient, this is not possible. The damage to the connections from the sympathetic nervous system does not allow this to happen. The heart may race, the blood vessels may dilate, and other things that are supposed to happen do, but not correctly or all together, so the blood pressure cannot be stabilized. So, going from sitting to more upright, to standing slowly can help. Always have something or someone to hold on to or to hold on to the patient. Sitting down or lying down again will raise the pressure quickly if necessary. Going slowly, with assistance is the key.

I can see now this is going to be an extensive and long process. I cannot give the information I want to give quickly. So, this is now part 1 of what will be a multi-post process. Let me know if there are subjects or symptoms you would like me to address. I will try to do so. Your own tips and thoughts are welcomed as well.

As you can see, I quickly realized that if I included all the tips and solutions we had found in one post, it would have been very long and involved. The above is the first of three as I said. Here is number two:

Monday, March 28, 2011

Maybe this will help - Part 2

A problem with the way these blogs work will mean the "end" of these posts will be first. But, it is what it is. Here is post #2 on my wife's symptoms and what if anything we were able to do to help.

The second symptom that manifested itself in the onset of my wife's disease path was Parkinson's-type tremors and rigidity as well as loss of fine motor skills. I put these all together for convenience of discussion. But maybe some background is in order.

MSA is a disease that was designated to cover what was three distinct diseases - Shy-Drager syndrome, striatonigral degeneration, and olivopontocerebellar atrophy.

In Shy-Drager syndrome, the most prominent symptoms are those involving the autonomic system, the body system that regulates blood pressure, urinary function, and other functions not involving conscious control. Olivopontocerebellar atrophy principally affects balance, coordination, and speech. These two are now usually classified as MSA-C subtype. (although some "experts" classify them separately)

Striatonigral degeneration causes parkinsonian symptoms such as slowed movements and rigidity, as well as the tremors that most people recognize as Parkinson's. This is known as MSA-P.

My wife has symptoms of both (or all three) types. At some point most MSA patients do show symptoms of both. The main distiquishing factor in the classification is the patients response (or lack thereof) to levadopa or other typical medicines used to treat Parkinson's. Luckily, my wife does respond to levadopa for her tremors and rigidity. This helps with those symptoms.

Loss of fine motor skills and tremors are particularly annoying to the patient (and caregiver?). This takes away most of the day to day skills that we all take for granted. Feeding ones self, brushing ones teeth, writing, using a keyboard, working the remote control, dialing a phone, and more. My wife is unable to do any of these currently and has not for a while.

To help with these Parkinson's type symptoms, parkinson-type tools and medicines may help. There are a world of utensils and devices for parkinson's patients. We found most of them too late (hence these posts). There is silverware with large weighted and/or padded handles. A patient with tremors can hold and use these when traditional silverware becomes unusable. There are divided and weighted plates to help in getting food on the silverware. There are plate guards to put on the edge of "real" plates to do the same. We used this when we would go out and my wife wanted to feed herself and not use a divided plate. For writing, the larger padded pens are the best. The larger, heavier, and padded items in all these cases are the best. You can "google" this and get many, many references to sites and companies that offer all of this and more. If you live in a larger populated area you should have a medical supply store that offers some or all. We found the online places to be more convenient and cheaper, but to each his own.

There are simple tips like always get a "to go" cup and straw, or bring your own travel cup/mug. We have a collection of them. We knocked over a few glassed before this one dawned on us. When food comes, it requires cutting - go ahead and do it. Trying to reach over and cut a bite or two every so often is more disruptive (at least to us) than just taking the plate and doing what needs to be done at the beginning. There are "bibs" or aprons that can be put on, similar to a lobster bib that restaurants use for diners. If you do not want to look like the patient is wearing a bib, at least tuck the napkin into the collar. We ruined a few shirts/blouses before we started using one of these at most meals.

One last thing. Do go out. Do try to live as normal a life (see previous posts, there is no normal!) as possible. One aspect of this damned disease is - it will all become very, very difficult if not impossible at some point. Do what you can when you can. To the caregivers - if cutting food, giving drinks, and feeding your patient offends you - get a helper. We went through a period where we did not want to go anywhere because it was hard, or my wife would be embarrassed at being fed, or whatever. You deserve to live - so live!

More to come. Comments, questions, and suggestions are welcomed.

I later decided that I needed three posts. You can tell at the end of this last post I thought I was done. However, I remembered that I had not covered one of the most prevalent issues/symptoms that plagued Carol and most MSA patients. Here is the third post:

Tuesday, March 29, 2011
Maybe this will help - part 3

THIS IS PART 3 OF A SERIES OF POSTS I DID THAT COVER MY WIFE'S SYMPTOMS AND THINGS WE DID (OR LEARNED) TO HELP. I NOTICED THAT THIS ONE GETS READ SIX OR SEVEN TIMES MORE THAN THE OTHER TWO. IF YOU OR A LOVED ONE ARE SUFFERING FROM MSA (or a similar disease) I HIGHLY RECOMMEND YOU READ THE OTHER TWO AS WELL. THESE ARE THINGS THAT I WISH WE HAD KNOWN IN OUR JOURNEY. Scott 12/15/12

Here we go again with symptoms and complications of my wife's MSA (Multiple System Atrophy for those of you not playing along).

I thought of this one when I was writing yesterday's post. It actually started before all the others, but in a non-intrusive way. (plus I was not involved at that point) I am talking about incontinence.

Urogentital problems are some of the first to show up in most MSA patients. Bladder leakage, especially in women, erection problems in men; and the host of other "plumbing" issues that can occur - usually do.
For those of you that are not on the north side of 50 or females without multiple pregnancies and birth, you may not realize that these problems are quite common among those that do fit into these categories. Therefore the onset of these symptoms is not attached to MSA until MSA attaches itself, in most cases.

We have six children. For those of you who still look for storks or go to the cabbage patch, that means my wife carried and delivered six little people. That takes a toll on the body, especially in the area of discussion here. As most men are, I was ignorant of this fact. I did not know that most women over the age of 40 pee when they sneeze or laugh. (note to women - you guys have done a wonderful job of coverup. But, you need to stop the Poise people. They are blowing it for you!) My wife had been having some "leakage" problems for a while. The move to incontinence was and is a gradual one. MSA speeds this process up, dramatically in some cases.

We do not have any secrets here. I can highly recommend the undergarment products sold by Wal-Mart sold under the Assurance brand. They are of a good quality. They work as needed. They are much less money than the name brand stuff like Depends. Tena makes a good incontinence pad. They have a nighttime version that again, really works. It is also less money than the Poise. In our experience, it actually works better.

There are bed pads that can be used for chairs as well as beds. I can tell you, in our experience, the lower priced ones here are fine. They are a backup anyway. I would advise you to put one under the sheets as a backup. We have saved the mattress a few times with this one. If no accidents occur, you just leave it when you change the sheets. One other note - always travel with a backup pad/brief or any other products you use. You never know. (there is a post I did called - "To pee or not to pee" that goes into this")

My wife has also gotten some help from medicine. She takes a product called Sanctura, the extended release version. She has been on it for over a year now. Although we would have to take her off it to see what exactly it is doing now, we did notice a marked improvement when she started. Her "control" is better now than is was when we started as well. It has the side benefit of being an anticholinergic. This class of drugs was used to treat Parkinson's symptoms before the discovery and use of Levadopa. So, in addition to helping with her bladder problems it seems to help somewhat with the parkinsonism aspect of her disease. There are other better known products for bladder control. You may see some commercials on TV. The reason for this one, we were told, is the fact that it does not affect the brain function. My wife has the curse of participating in most negative side effects of drugs. Other bladder control medicines seemed to bother her more than this. Other than a dry mouth, this one seems fine. You and your doctor would have to find the best for you. I would recommend you put Sanctura on your list however.

Beyond making you aware of the medicines, the incontinence products aisle that is now in almost any full-line retailer, and the products we have found to be the best deal; I would want to remind you of an important point. DO NOT TRY TO CONTROL INCONTINENCE BY LIMITING FLUIDS!! With the orthostatic hypotension that is prevelant among most MSA patients, it is critical to remain fully hydrated. My wife was trying to control her "leakage" early in this process with the result that she was passing out more often. Not a good trade off. Drink liquids - as much as you can. The benefits outweigh the negatives.

As the title says - Maybe this will help.

CHAPTER TWENTY-TWO

A Vision

I write a lot of poetry and always have. Especially when I am emotionally invested in something or someone, poetry just comes to me. This is one that came to me when looking at Carol one evening.

Wednesday, April 27, 2011

Visions

I see you sometimes as you were

laughing, not crying.

walking, not lying.

doing, not trying.

living, not dying.

I see you mostly as you are

sitting, not walking.

quiet, not talking.

with death stalking.

But,

I see you sometimes as you were

"THE" 4/27/11

It chills me when I look and see that almost exactly a month later (May 28th) we would be loading Carol into the back of an ambulance.

CHAPTER TWENTY-THREE

GRASPING AT STRAWS

We had pretty good insurance, but we still had a LOT of medical bills that our insurance would not pay. That is because we did some things that insurance did not think were medically necessary or were considered too experimental to pay for. Now, if you have a loved one that is dying, and someone offers a reasonable treatment, you go for it. The cost was not a high priority. One thing we investigated on several occasions was stem cell therapy. Every now and then you would come across a patient that would report tremendous results from stem cell treatment, especially in China. I corresponded with a number of doctors in China, Venezuela, Canada, and the USA. I could find no credible evidence that any of them offered any true improvement in symptoms beyond the short term. There were also family members I spoke to that had their loved ones die after one of these treatments. People that know me know that I am a bear when it comes to researching something that I want to find out about. I spent a LOT of time researching stem cell treatments. I do think stem cell therapy and treatments offer tremendous opportunities for treating many diseases. I think the field will have great advances in the future. After researching and talking to doctors, patients, and family members of patients, I wrote the post below outlining my thoughts.

Sunday, May 1, 2011

Stem Cell Treatment - my take

Everywhere you go on any MSA support or information site forum, you will find questions about stem cell treatment. I have done a LOT of research on stem cell treatment, especially as it relates to MSA and/or the cerebellum and medulla. Here is what I have found.

Stem cell treatment is not an approved therapy in the U.S. for most applications. It is still in the research stage in most areas that it has been approved for at this writing. There are some amazing results in very specific instances. The reasons for stem cell therapy not being approved are many, some of which are idiotic (in my opinion) protests for religious or moral reasons. That is another topic for later. Stem cell treatments are not approved for mainstream applications yet because they have not been proven safe or effective. I think some day stem cell treatment will be of great benefit, especially in certain diseases or traumatic injury. I do NOT think MSA will be one of them. Here is why.

Stem cell therapy works by inserting stem cells into a damaged area. Stem cells have the ability to recreate any cell in the body. Where cellular degeneration is involved, this can be a miracle just waiting to happen. MSA, and some other degenerative neurological diseases, involve a destruction of brain tissue especially in the medulla and cerebellum. The dopamine receptors are also specifically targeted by the disease. A bit of background (a disclaimer - I am not a doctor or trained in medicine. I read a LOT and have spoken at detail with a LOT of neurologists. This is not meant to be a scientific dissertation, just informative. I am sure there are mistakes, hopefully none of a major variety. Feel free to correct me.) - in Parkinson's the body's ability to produce dopamine and certain other neurogenic transmitters is compromised (or halted). The receptors and mechanisms to utilize the neuro-transmitters is still intact in most cases. That is why supplementation with L-Dopa is usually effective, especially in the early stages of the disease. In MSA the dopaminic receptors are damaged/destroyed. That is why a large number of MSA patients do not respond to dopamine supplementation. There is no system by which it can be utilized no matter how much is there.

Now the reason for stem cell treatment not working in MSA. The mechanism by which the dopamine receptors and brain tissue is being destroyed is not known. If (and it is a big IF) stem cell therapy were to regenerate the receptors and/or the brain tissue, it would be destroyed again. How about an example - you buy an old house. A few years in you start having electrical problems. You call an electrician and he says you have frayed wiring that is shorting out. You have him replace the wires. Months later you start having the problems again. The electrician comes out and says your wires are frayed again. You find there is something eating at the wires. You know the electrician can replace the wires again. However, even if you completely rewire the house the problem will continue until you find and eliminate whatever is eating at your wiring. (I know, call an exterminator. Easy - but try to find an exterminator that will work in the human brain on an unknown vermin!) MSA has unknown vermin eating at the wiring of the brain. All the replacing in the world will not solve the problem.

There are risks involved in stem cell therapy. There are immense costs involved, not the least of which travel to a foreign country is involved. In my opinion, after extensive research; there is no benefit to MSA patients that outweigh those risks and costs. It would appear the best you could hope for is a short reprieve from some of the symptoms.

Believe me I know first hand how frustrating this disease can be with it's relentless decline, clueless medical personnel, and lack of treatment. I just do not see stem cell treatment as any part of the answer, at least at this stage of development.

FYI, this is one of the most read posts on the blog. I am not sure if it is just the stem cell title that draws people in or if it is MSA patients desperately searching for something that will help; as we were.

CHAPTER TWENTY-FOUR

PARTING IS SUCH SWEET SORROW

As it turned out, somewhat ironically, I might add, this post was done less than thirty days before Carol died. I was commenting on how meeting patients with MSA was hard as they were all terminal. Two of the families/patients I was corresponding with had passed away in the recent days prior to this. I was lamenting that fact.

Saturday, May 7, 2011

Watch what you wish for...

I know most if not all of you have heard the expression - "Watch what you wish for. You just might get it" (or similar). I can attest this is true.

During the time my wife and I have been dealing with this disease, I have often commented on the lack of interaction and contact between people dealing with it. With an estimated 4.6 people per 100,000 population, that does not give a large group to interact with. My wife and I are yet to meet in person another patient with MSA, except for a MSA national conference and support meeting we went to a few years ago. This was in Tennessee (we live in N.C.), "promoted" nationally, and even at this event there were only ten or twelve patients.

Through this blog, my other "all purpose blog", Facebook, and the various forums on MSA support and awareness pages; I have made contact and "met" eight or nine patients or caregivers of patients with MSA over the past six months or so. It has been great to communicate, even distantly, with people that can share and understand exactly what you are going through.

Now for the downside and the reason for the title of this disease. In the six months or so I have "known" these people, two of the people afflicted with this terrible disease have succumbed to it.
The contact I was wishing for (and enjoyed when it occurred) becomes itself a reminder of how insidious and relentless this damned disease is. One fourth of the people I have "met" that have this disease have died within six months of our first contact!

Damn I hate this disease. Bless everyone that is suffering from it - patients, family, and friends - even those that only meet like this.

As I said above, Carol was to succumb to this terrible disease less than a month later. These next posts are from the hospital and after.

CHAPTER TWENTY-FIVE

HELL ON EARTH

This one was written in the wee hours of the morning after Carol had been taken by ambulance to the hospital. I am pretty sure it requires no more explaining than that.

Sunday, May 29, 2011

There is a Hell!

Regardless of your belief in Heaven and Hell, I can assure you without a doubt - there IS a Hell! This is not a hell of fire and brimstone. This is not a hell of evildoers or non-believers that I am speaking of. It is a hell of doubts and second guesses. It is a hell of what-ifs, and whys? It is a hell of alarms and cords, tubing and needles. It is not a hell of below - it is a hell of here on earth.

MSA is a hell. The consequences of MSA and other alphabet diseases are HELL!

The flesh is temporary. LOVE is eternal.

We are powerless over MSA. MSA is powerless over LOVE.

I want to send out hugs, kisses, and LOVE to any and all afflicted with this DAMNED disease.

Peace be with you.

I wrote this on my phone sitting in a waiting room with my children. Carol had not officially been pronounced dead but was non-responsive and on a respirator. I had just signed a DNR per Carol's wishes and was dealing with all the feelings that brought on as well as dealing with our children and their lack of understanding as to why I would sign the DNR.

Let me fill you in on a little background of the hours prior to this. Saturday May 28th, 2011 was another day in MSA wonderland. Nothing special or different. Carol had been in the hospital in March and had been on a PICC line for antibiotic treatment well into early May. She had some issues with recovery and had not felt particularly well since, but nothing major. My youngest daughter had left a bit earlier to go out and Carol and I were watching "Swamp People" on TV. It was one that had a lot of idiotic mess-ups in it and we had both laughed most of the hour it was on. After it was over, I asked her if she was ready to go to bed. She said, "give me a minute". I asked if she was OK and she just said she wanted to sit for a moment. So, we sat. In about 10 minutes she said she was ready. I got her in her wheelchair and we headed back. The bathroom had been a particular nemesis during her recovery from the infection as the transition from chair to toilet and the other activities there seemed to cause her to pass out much more than prior to the infection. Sure enough, she passed out. Now, I was not too alarmed as it had happened frequently over the past two weeks. However, all the tricks I usually did were not bringing her back. I knew I was on the clock as her breathing had stopped (also normal, but it always came back after a few missed breaths). I yelled in her ear – "wake up or I am calling 911". My phone was in the other room, so I threw her over my shoulder and carried her into our bedroom, put her on the bed, and called 911. I also started chest compressions. I got the dispatcher on the phone and explained what was going on. I also gave her a quick "lesson" on MSA and what the EMTs would find when they got to me. She told me to start chest compressions and I explained I had been doing them while we were on the phone. So, I did chest compressions (I switched to full CPR after about two minutes as I knew the oxygen levels in Carol's blood would be low at this point). This went on for about eight minutes. I head the ambulance and fire truck pull up outside and someone at the door. Now, with my daughter out I had not locked the front door – thankfully – so I yelled for them to come in and that we were in the back of the house. They came back and immediately took over. I was explaining what had happened, the timeline, what I had done, and a bit about MSA to them. They bagged Carol and used a defibrillator to get her heart going. Then they readied her for transport and I started calling my children. I followed the ambulance to the hospital. I want to take this opportunity to thank the Winston-Salem/Forsyth County fire department and Ambulance services for their professionalism and quick response. They were better than I could have expected, especially considering the circumstances.

I found out later that Carol coded twice on the way to the hospital. With that being about a fifteen-minute drive, that was not good at all. I found this out after I signed the DNR, but it helped me to know that later to help justify the futility of trying to resuscitate her. At the hospital they got her heart stabilized and had her on a respirator. She was totally non-responsive however.

We spend the next almost 48 hours in the hospital waiting for an official word.

CHAPTER TWENTY-SIX

IT IS OVER, YET IT BEGINS

The official date of Carol's death was May 31st, 2011. This was written shortly after the doctors performed another brain function test to see if there was activity. I already had determined Carol was gone. The last visit I had with her "felt" different. I am not sure which of the kids I told, but I remember saying, "she's not in there any more".

Legally, morally, and with a tiny gasp of hope; we all waited for the tests to be completed. It was official, Carol's battle with MSA and its assorted side-kicks was over. This was also written on my phone in the hospital.

Tuesday, May 31, 2011

Melted

If the sun and sky is dimmer it is because the light of my life went out! I will always love you!

To Carol:

I will always live with what I did and did not do. I am profoundly saddened by my inability to do all you needed. It was not from lack of concern, effort. or love. Our 38 years+ was WAY too short. You were the yin to my yang. I am left with a hole in my heart that cannot heal. Thanks for leaving part of you here with me in our six great children. They salve my wound.

Snow always melts!

The 36+ hours straight in the hospital had drained me and all the family more than I can express. I was mentally and physically shot as were all of the others. Carol had requested that any of her organs that could be successfully used for transplants be used, so that was one of the decisions made. The hospital staff all lined the hall as they took her from the room to the OR for harvesting. It was a great show of respect that meant a lot to all of us. I was later shocked to find the show of respect was done somewhat due to the fact that not very many people do the organ donations. I am amazed by that, but to each his own I guess. I would like to put out an appeal to all: become an organ donor. If some part of you can help someone, why not? If you think you are keeping the integrity of the body, ask about the embalming process. Why not have the body that is not being used any longer do some good?

This was an end, but it also was a beginning of a whirlwind of decisions, questions, forms, purchases, planning, and complications that I was not prepared for. As I mentioned in earlier posts and comments, discussions of Carol's ultimate demise never happened. The elephant visited us often, but we ignored him with great ease. I will make another appeal, do some planning. Make your final wishes known. It is hard, but it is a kindness to those left behind.

CHAPTER TWENTY-SEVEN

A POEM

This short poem came to me as I was headed home from the hospital. I have always liked it.

Tuesday, May 31, 2011

Eternal

The essence of someone

is held in the memories

and bound by love

always to remain.

People are eternal

if they are remembered with love.

R.I.P. Carol
"THE" 5/31/11

As mentioned earlier, I write a lot of poetry, and always have. The poems just come to me, especially when emotions are running high. There are more to come. There are countless numbers I have never published anywhere, many I have written for others, and countless more I have never even written down. Maybe a book of poetry someday...

CHAPTER TWENTY-EIGHT

CALL THE NEWSPAPERS

Carol's obituary was another thing that we had not discussed. I read a few and looked at the format and then wrote this the day after she died. It ran the next day in several newspapers. Speaking of newspapers, one thing I learned and was shocked by was the price of running an obituary. My wife was from the Ft. Lauderdale, Florida area. We were going to run her obituary in the Ft. Lauderdale paper. I say were because they wanted over $500 to run it! (in 2011!)

Thursday, June 2, 2011

Obituary

Carol's obituary -

Carol Poole

Carol J. Condon Poole of Winston-Salem, 56 left her wheelchair behind forever Monday May 30th after more than five years battling MSA (multiple system atrophy). She departed after a final selfless act of organ donation with her loving family by her side.

Carol was born in Pennsylvania to Marlen Condon but grew up a true Florida girl in Plantation, Florida. After graduating from Plantation High School Carol attended Western Carolina University where she met her husband-to-be. After becoming a certified operating room technician at Presbyterian Hospital in Charlotte, N.C., she went on to become a R.N. Carol was retired on disability from Forsyth Medical Center where she worked in the operating room for over ten years. Carol was known at work for her compassion, professionalism, and sense of humor.

After WCU, Scott Poole and Carol were married. On May 16th they celebrated 38 years together as husband and wife. Carol was a loving mother of six children – Christi Waiters, Kimberly Bowers, David Poole, Stephani Poole, Patrick Poole, and Bailey Poole; and a grandmother to Hannah Byerly, Landon Byerly, and Alyson Bowers, all of the greater Winston-Salem area. She was a doting Mom and Nana to all. Her love as a wife, mother and grandmother was endless.

Carol is survived by her above mentioned family as well as her mother Marlen Condon of The Villages, Florida, and her twin sister Karen Parsons and her family of Summerville, S.C

Carol's life will be celebrated on Thursday June 2nd at the Regency Ballroom of the Quality Inn & Suites 2008 S. Hawthorne Road. W-S N.C. from 6:30 – 8:30 pm. All that knew her are asked to come and share your memories and listen to others share theirs. Food and beverages will be provided. Dress as you wish.

In lieu of flowers, please send donations to:

Team Carol

c/o Trinity Center

640 Holly Avenue

Winston-Salem, N.C. 27101

You will notice that I mentioned sending donations to the Trinity Center. This is how they describe themselves on their webpage at https://www.trinitycenterinc.com/

an ecumenical center for counseling, spiritual

formation, and education.

I do not know the folks there now, like most things – change happens. People come and go. I will say that Trinity Center offered Carol counseling and assistance with her state of mind was of immense help to her (and myself).

CHAPTER TWENTY-NINE

ANOTHER POEM

Saturday, June 4, 2011
TEARS
As I wipe my eyes again
I know,
I'll never be the same.
I think I'm done,
but they can well back up
whenever I hear your name.
Sure
I laugh at things.
But it's more for them than me.
I wonder if life will ever seem
the way it used to be.

"THE" 6/3/11

CHAPTER THIRTY

MAKING SOME SENSE OF IT ALL

Humans always try to make sense of senseless acts and happenings. A death, no matter how expected, is one of them. I wanted to try to have people realize what I took away from Carol's illness and subsequent death.

Sunday, June 5, 2011

Laugh, Live, and LOVE

This past week has been a surreal experience. I have had the unfortunate experience to lose many family members over the years including my father, but nothing has been close to this. I have had many, many thoughts - as I have stated here before, I am more "creative" when emotional (as you can see in the previous posts from the past seven days).

Here are some thoughts on life:

Probably the biggest advice/most important thing I can pass along is almost a tired cliché - live every day as it is your (or your loved one's) last day. Although my wife had a terminal illness, I thought we had time to do and say what we wanted. If you have something you have always wanted to do, if there is any way you can do it (or a close substitute) financially - I recommend you DO IT! If there is something you want to say - same advice - SAY IT! Besides the loss of my lifetime companion, things left undone or unsaid are the hardest for me. This is especially true if these things are simple things. You may want to go for ice cream. If you are a caregiver for someone that cannot move well, that can be hard. It is easier to say to yourself (or your loved one) - "We will do that tomorrow". I used to tell my kids (in fact we had a little chant that I bet they remember) - *tomorrow never comes*. By definition that is true - yesterday's tomorrow is today. So, waiting for tomorrow is fruitless in many ways.

Try to find something to laugh at. This one was probably one of the things that my wife and I did the best. She had a great sense of humor and I and am a renown idiot. I do remember we laughed at many things last Saturday (her last day conscious). I am very glad for that. Oh, there were days we wept togther as well. I feel that is important too, but laughter is great for everyone involved. Try to find something that can make you laugh, as often as you can.

Involve family and friends. I feel my wife and I left this one a bit short. It was so easy for us to withdraw and just have each other. That is great, but it means two people are trying to "recharge" each other. When you get run down and depressed, that can be impossible. I believe the most important thing you get by contact with people that love you, and you love, is strength. We all need to be recharged with love, faith, and friendship to make it. Our internal "batteries" can only go so long without a charge. Like I said, if both of you are low on "juice" that will not happen. You are running on empty. The first two points above can help recharge to a point, but ultimately you need other people to pull the "power" from. Our kids and family were close, but see point one - everyone thinks there is going to be a tomorrow to visit. If you are the caregiver, remember YOU need recharging. This is probably the area that I was most remiss in. I felt like I needed to be with my wife every moment I could. Don't get me wrong, I am grateful for every minute. But, going back to point one, I wonder if I had stepped away occasionally if I would have had the strength (or drive, or gumption, or whatever) to take my wife out more, even if it was just to ride around. Caregivers, take care of yourself. I know I am not the first to say that by any means, but it is important enough to repeat often.

Tell those you love that you love them - do it often. Then repeat. 'Nuff said.

As a follow up (and maybe conclusion) to the above points I will get personal again. We have had family and friends around all week. We have had food enough to feed small countries. We have cried together and we have laughed together. All of that has been wonderful; in fact, I do not know how I would have made it through the week without it. However, my wife (and I) would have LOVED to have the people, the food, and the fellowship when she was alive. If you know someone that is suffering with an illness, especially if they are limited in movement - go see them! If they are family, you are REQUIRED to! Any of the gatherings we have had this week, had they happened last anytime in the previous weeks, would have thrilled my wife (and me) to no end. If you know a family that is going through something like mine just did, take them a meal or a dessert. Drop them a call. Send them a card. Offer to go shopping for them. I am lucky in that I have six children that all live fairly close by and they helped me with this, but we still did not get everyone together and commune like we have this past week. Like I said, my wife would have loved it, as I am sure most people in her condition would have. Make a point to contact them.

Enough for now. I realize I got a bit "preachy". Sorry. I do feel strongly about this for obvious reasons. I hope I can live up to my own words as I go forward.

There is a lot of emotion contained within those words. As I read them now I realize that I probably have not lived up to my own words, at least not as well as I had hoped. Well, as long as I have another day I can keep working at it. I recommend you do the same.

CHAPTER THIRTY-ONE

IT IS NEVER REALLY OVER

I was, and continue to be, amazed at the outpouring of support and kindness that was sent to me after Carol's passing via email and otherwise, from the blog posts.

Sunday, June 12, 2011
Thanks
I wanted to take a moment to thank all the people from around the world that offered their condolences. I greatly appreciate your thoughts and prayers. The pain has been made easier to bear by the kind words.

I am not sure yet what I am going to do with this blog. I will see. If anyone has any questions or thoughts they would like to share or ask, please do so.

My best to any and all afflicted with or affected by this horrible disease (or any of the alphabet diseases).

Again, thanks,

Scott

The next two are along the same vein of thought. Even almost three months later the emails and condolences continued to come in from people I have never met. This was one I wrote after getting a particularly kind email from a family member of a patient with MSA.

Saturday, August 13, 2011
The aftermath - a follow up
It was 11 weeks from when I am writing this that the ambulance took my wife away. It was 11 weeks ago that I last spoke to her. It was 11

weeks ago that I was doing chest compressions for 8+ long minutes waiting for the ambulance to arrive. In a way it seems like yesterday. In other ways it seems a lifetime ago.

I am still amazed at the views this blog gets. I am more amazed at the comments. I am extremely grateful for the kind words and thoughts that have been sent my way. I am gratified by the fact that people find some help, information, and attachment here and then take the time to comment on it. As rare as MSA is, there are way too many families out there that are facing this terrible nightmare of a disease. That is the main reason I am posting now. I feel somewhat obligated to do so. However, I gladly would do so every day if I thought I could offer any comfort or help to anyone dealing with this disease (or any of the alphabet diseases).

Even though the diagnosis of MSA is a death sentence, (sorry if that is harsh to anyone reading this that has not accepted this, but unfortunately it is true - at least now) it is so hard facing the end. I am surprised every day at how the loss of my wife is still so raw. In my case I think one of the things that made/makes it so hard is the fact that my wife just "left". I always saw the end as a more gradual thing. Maybe hospice in a bed, surrounded by loved ones, and saying goodbye. My wife passed out and never woke back up. Even though we said our goodbyes, it was not at all what was envisioned. She was not able to say goodbye back. In a way this is a good thing. One of my wife's biggest fears and concerns was a feeding tube, a catheter, and a long drawn out ordeal. I know my wife's condition made her miserable. The inability to communicate was one of her biggest frustrations. She could not speak well at all, with no volume. That make the phone impossible to use. She could not type on her computer due to the tremors and lack of motor control. She was isolated from all those she loved, to a point even those in the same room. I have posts on this site about how many times I said "what?", "excuse me?", or just "huh?". There were a lot of times that she would just say never mind and give up. From that perspective the way things went was definitely for the better. From a "closure" perspective, it was far from perfect; at least for us left here.

I find the days getting easier to deal with. I know this is a good thing. I know this is the natural course. I also know that in a way it makes me feel guilty. It seems like not feeling so sad is not fair to her. But again, I know that a life with nothing but profound sadness is not much of a life at all. I also know with all my heart that she would not want me to be very sad all the time. Every one of us here on earth now will be dead at some point. This is the case with every person that has or ever will live. It is still hard to deal with when it hits you.

The thing that gets me the most is music. I can hear a song from our past, particularly the early days of our relationship, and be hit with a flood of emotions and memories. I still find myself thinking I will have to tell her about something I have seen or heard when I get home that night. Being together for almost 39 years and married for 38+ develops a real attachment at multiple levels. To lose that connection is weird and very difficult to do without. The longest we were apart for those 38+ years was less than a week. To now be at 11 weeks without seeing her or talking to her is still very odd and discomforting.

I will post here when I have something to say. I do check the comments and try to answer anyone that gives me a contact with a question or a request for contact. I do think daily of those that I have "met" through this blog, Facebook, and some other MSA-related sites. I would still love to hear from anyone that wants to drop me an email, a comment, or a question. I welcome any of you with questions to look at the three posts here entitled - "Maybe this will help..." parts 1, 2, and 3. They are a synopsis of my wife's symptoms and how we dealt with them.

Until later.

Songs are still the hardest for me, particularly ones that Carol and I would listen to in our earlier lives. In fact, I do not listen to a lot of music still today due to the fact that it can affect me so strongly. As I have mentioned, I still get the occasional email or comment on the blog from a family member or patient thanking me for the information in the blog or offering condolences. That is very heartwarming. I truly hope the blog, and now possibly this book, can offer some help to people that are travelling this path.

And it continued to amaze me:

Monday, November 7, 2011
They just keep coming!
Last month - October 2011 - logged the second highest number of
visits to this blog in its existence. As I have stated before, I am
constantly amazed at the number of hits this site still gets. I feel kind
of bad since I hardly ever post here anymore, so here I am.

Hardly a week goes by without me getting an email or a comment
from someone expressing their good wishes/blessings on me and my
family or to thank me for writing the posts I did. That is extremely
gratifying. As I said when I started this, this blog was for me -
especially when it started. I will admit as I talked to and "met" other
people with MSA I did get some inspiration to try to offer some posts
that I thought might help those going through the hell that is a
degenerative neurological disease.

I have noticed that the second most popular post here is my post
about stem cell treatments. I understand this as one of the great
agonies of MSA is the lack of treatment. I am doing more research
now and will do an additional post when I feel I have anything new to
add. For now I stick by the recommendation of the original post -
stem cell treatment, especially since it involves extensive cost and
travel, is not something I feel is worth it. It also could be very
dangerous. The hospitals that are doing the procedure are not under
any medical protocol approvals like we are used to here in the U.S. It
is still very much an experimental procedure. I do not want to take
away hope from anyone. I definitely know the burning desire to do
SOMETHING to try to beat back this evil malady. I also recognize that
I am only giving my opinion. However, it is an educated opinion. I
have spent many hours researching the stem cell procedures that are
out there now. I have even had two email "conversations" with
Doctors in China that work in facilities that do the procedures. (both
told me, "off the record" that they would not have the procedure
done on themselves or a loved one with MSA - FYI) So, I will revisit
this sometime in the next six months.

I am still upset by the lack of views the posts "Maybe this will help"
parts 1-3 get. Those contain things I wish I had been told when my
wife and I were going through the daily trials and challenges of MSA. I
recommend you read these if you are a caregiver. I am not claiming
to have all the answers. Heck, I don't even have all the questions.
What I tried to do was tell you what we faced, and some of the ways

we made it better. If the MSA advances for you like it did for us, knowing ahead of time can be a great help. A lot of our "fixes" we came up with only worked for us for a very short time due to the progression of the symptoms.

I wish everyone affected by MSA my best. Family members, patients, medical staff dealing with the symptoms, researchers working on finding out what exactly is going on with the disease and hopefully working on a cure are all in my thoughts. Best wishes and good luck to all of you. Please feel free to comment or write me
- gumbypoole@aol.com

Holidays are hard for survivors. We are struck with memories and rituals that are so deeply tied to the missing that it is a physical hurt, particularly the first ones. The first of lots of things are hard — birthdays, anniversaries, Christmases, New Year's, etc. are a reminder of what was. My first Christmas in almost four decades without Carol definitely qualified as hard. I was thinking about it a lot a week before Christmas.

Happy Holidays, Merry Christmas, and Happy New Year!!

Well, one week from now, as I am writing this, the first Christmas without my wife in 38 years will be over. I will admit I am not looking forward to it (except for the grandkids). Christmas, heck holidays in general, was/were my wife's "thing". We shall see what happens.

I wanted to take this time to wish anyone affected by or afflicted with this disease a very Merry Christmas, Happy Holidays, and a very Happy New Year. To family members that are dealing with or caring for patients and in memory of those that have lost their battle with MSA as well. I have a saying that I have shared with people and try to live by - Have as good a day as you can have.

I am still getting a phenomenal number of hits to this site. Not a week has gone by that I have not gotten multiple emails from people with MSA or family members of patients that are desperately looking for some consolation, advice, or just someone to listen. I answer everyone gladly. I remember how desperate I was with my wife. I told her and felt many times that the disease was "outrunning" us. As I have stated on other posts here, every time we would come up with a "solution" to an aspect of the disease, the progression of the the disease took us on to another one. To all of you reading this for the first time, or that have not read many posts here; please go to the posts entitled "Maybe this will help.." parts 1, 2, and 3. These posts are a synopsis of my wife's symptoms, their progression, and the "solutions" we came up with to deal with them.

I look forward to hearing from any and all of you. gumbypoole@aol.com

Then on Christmas day it did hit hard. I wrote this:

Sunday, December 25, 2011

What would you do...?

What would you do differently today if you knew it was your last Christmas? Or the last Christmas of a loved one? A good friend?

Even though my wife had a terminal illness, we did not think last Christmas was our last together. We were just weeks back from a cruise, she was feeling pretty good (for her). Who knew?

So, who would you call? Who would you visit? Who would you hug? Who would you kiss?
What would you do? What would you eat, say, buy, sell, give away, hold, or ignore?

We don't know, do we? DO IT!!

Merry Christmas!

CHAPTER THIRTY-THREE

BY POPULAR DEMAND

I mentioned in one of the earlier posts that the stem cell "report" I did was (and is) one of the most read posts on the blog. People are desperately searching for a cure or at least a remission. If you search the internet for almost any disease with a terminal outcome stem cell therapy will come up. There are supposed "patients" (I say supposed and quotes because when I tried to contact these folks I was only able to find one), supposed Doctors (again, the ones making the claims are hard to have a true scientific discussion with), or family members. I did get one patient that traded a few emails with me. He said he and his wife had gone to China. He and I first corresponded when he was recovering from the treatment back here in the USA, about two months in if my memory serves. He said that there may have been a bit of an improvement in movement and lack of tremors at that point. I heard from him about a month later and he told me he walked unaided for the first time in years. A month after that he was ecstatic, he said he was speaking more clearly, able to eat more foods, and moving better than he had in a long, long time. Then six months or so after that he wrote me an email saying he was going back downhill and had gone back to using a cane. His wife wrote me a few months later and said he was bed-ridden. About a year later she wrote and said he had passed away a month prior of a lung infection. He had been bed-ridden since our previous contact. I did a lot of research into the newer techniques of stem cell therapy and this is what I wrote:

Sunday, January 22, 2012
Stem Cells - follow up
Before I get into the topic I again want to express my astonishment over the hits this site is still getting, as well as the comments and emails I get. To say I enjoy them would be wrong, because it usually means I am "meeting" another person suffering with MSA. However, it is always good to hear from people. I am grateful when this site is

mentioned as offering some support and/or solace. Please feel free to comment or contact me.

The second most read post on this site is the one I did about stem cells (fyi, #1 is the intro page) If you have not read it, here it is: http://www.livingwithasnowman.blogspot.com/2011/05/stem-cell-treatment-my-take.html. I promised a follow up. I have been doing research and have contacted many people to gather as much information as I could. I do not mean for this to be the definitive stem cell comment by any means, but I do hope it will provide some support for those looking at the treatments. **At the end I have placed some links you may find helpful in your own journey.**

I have been argued with over my first post and the conclusions I came to that stem cell treatments for MSA, at least at this time, are a waste of money. I am sad to say I can find nothing to change my opinion at this writing. Stem cell treatment for MSA (or other alphabet diseases, especially of the CNS) is not proven to offer any lasting medical improvement, and has caused harm to some patients with complications such as infections, immune system responses (rejection), etc. There are inherent dangers with any medical procedure. Even a simple vaccination injection can be very dangerous in certain cases due to allergic reactions. It is rare, but it happens. To pay tens of thousands of dollars for an unproven, potentially deadly procedure with no proven record of safety or success is not a good bet, at least in my opinion.

I understand the allure of stem cell treatment (or other treatments with promises of curing or reversing these terrible diseases that standard medicine cannot help with). To accept that there are diseases that modern medicine cannot treat, much less cure, is very hard to do. My wife and I talked about stem cell treatments and other alternatives a lot. That is where I first became aware of the problems and dangers. I did hours and hours of research. I "spoke" to (either in person, on the phone, by email, or by mail) anyone that I could get up with that I thought had any knowledge of stem cell treatments. I mentioned in a post I did earlier, I even got two Chinese "doctors" (in quotes because one of them told me he was not a medical doctor, the clinic just referred to all their clinicians as "doctor") affiliated with a stem cell treatment center in China to tell me they would not use the treatments on their loved ones - it was too dangerous and did not work.

I do believe stem cell treatment offers a great resource for the treatment and possible cure of many, many diseases. I also believe we are many, many years away from this. I also believe that the treatment of CNS alphabet diseases may be the last frontier for these treatments, outside of spinal cord injury (there is a lot of promise there). Due to the fact that most of these alphabet diseases are not understood from a pathology or systemic standpoint, treatment is a long way off. The good news? A long way off in today's world can be much quicker than in the past. Advances in medical science are happening every day. There are discoveries being made as I write this. Maybe one of them will be able to offer treatment and/or further understanding of these diseases. For now my advice would be to stay away and save your money. If you are offered a chance to engage in stem cell research from an accredited research facility, go for it. They are probably not to the stage of a cure, but you may advance the field of study and treatment.

I promised links. Rather than clog things up with a lot of them, I have two. The first is for the ISSCR, the International Society for Stem Cell Research. They have a great site with a lot of information about what is going on in the stem cell research world. You can find their site here - http://www.closerlookatstemcells.org/. They also have many links there for you to continue your research. The second link is one I think I shared before. It is a link to a site that offers all the approved medical trials and studies going on in the U.S. It covers all diseases, but can be searched by specific disease. I have the link to the MSA and related studies. The link is
- http://clinicaltrials.gov/ct2/results?term=Multiple+System+Atrophy&recr=Open .

As always, have the best day you can have.

I have not followed up on stem cell treatments specifically for MSA or other Parkinson's Plus diseases, I will have to admit. I am not sure exactly what improvements, if any, have been made. I do believe stem cell therapy is very promising for a lot of diseases. Unless something has changed I am not aware of however, I do not see stem cells offering a "fix" or cure for a disease like MSA due to the actual "death" of the brain cells. It seem to me it is like putting air in a flat tire without fixing the hole. It just won't work. Again, I have NOT done any additional research into this since the above post.

CHAPTER THIRTY-FIVE

FILM FESTIVAL

One thing that is very frustrating about MSA and other rare diseases is the lack of understanding and awareness of what they are, even among the medical community. Although I have been somewhat chastised for not being as enamored with awareness for awareness' sake, I do understand that this is a problem. There came a chance for a film made by an MSA patient to win a contest through the American Academy of Neurology. I thought maybe I could assist in getting some votes.

Sunday, February 12, 2012

Please Help!

As most of you know, my wife passed away last May from a rare neurological disease called MSA. One of my goals in life is to offer support to those patients, caregivers, and families affected by this rare, fatal illness. The American Academy of Neurology has a film contest each year where they pick a short film made by individuals about support for brain disease research. Entries are submitted to You Tube and a winner is selected by popular vote. The film is then shown at the American Academy of Neurology annual meeting. This would really be important to help with MSA as it is very rare and still unknown to a lot of doctors and other medical personnel. I know this from personal experience. There is a film featuring a MSA patient that is entered in the contest this year. I would ask that you register, watch, and vote for the film. Even if you do not want to vote, please go watch the film. It will show you what MSA patients like my wife, go through with this illness.

Please help make Multiple System Atrophy film #1 at the Neuro Film Festival. A film on Multiple System Atrophy has been entered in the Neuro Film Festival.

We need your help to get enough votes to make it the "Fan Favorite", this will mean increased publicity for Multiple System Atrophy which is so desperately needed.

This is an achievable goal if we all work together.

As of February 11th, the film is in first place in the voting but the second-place film is very close behind, every single vote counts.

Ask your friends to vote, post on your Facebook wall and twitter accounts, get your teenage relatives involved so all their friends will vote too. We can do this!!!

PLEASE TAKE ACTION NOW! GO TO THIS WEBSITE AND ENTER YOUR VOTE BEFORE MARCH 8TH.

Please follow these instructions exactly to ensure your vote is counted

Step 1: Go to Neuro Film Festival Website
http://patients.aan.com/go/about/neurofilmfestival

Step 2: click on the VOTE NOW! tab.

Step 3: Click on Register Now and enter your details

Step 4: Check you email inbox for a verification email - click on the link to verify your registration

Step 5: Go Vote -- Go back to Neuro Film Festival Website
http://patients.aan.com/go/about/neurofilmfestival and click VOTE NOW

Step 6: Find the "Multiple System Atrophy MSA" film in the list and click on the word VOTE

Note: If you have more than one email address you may register that email and vote again.

One vote per registered email address.

Please do this and pass it on to everyone you can.

And it WORKED!!!

Saturday, March 17, 2012
Thanks to all!
This post will precede the post I am referring to, but if anyone has questions just go to next post (older).

The video featuring the MSA patient has won the Neuro Film Festival. It was a runaway in numbers. For all of you that voted, THANKS! Awareness of this (and other) rare neurological disease is greatly needed. Now all the attendees of the American Academy of Neurology annual meeting will see the video. I can tell you from experience that even neurologists are not always aware of the symptoms of MSA.

On a side note, although I am glad the MSA video won; and obviously I lobbied for the result - I am saddened to an extent by the fact that there were other videos there from just as dedicated family members, patients, and caregivers about other diseases that got almost no support/votes. Although I have a personal interest in promoting MSA awareness, I know ALL neurological diseases need attention, support, and research. I wish all those afflicted with and affected by these diseases the best. May treatments and cures be found for all.

CHAPTER THIRTY-SIX

ANNIVERSARY

I have written about how anniversaries, holidays, etc. are especially hard. Coming up on the first anniversary of Carol's death caused a lot of thoughts and memories to flow.

Wednesday, May 30, 2012
One Year Ago Today
I am actually writing this before I have a title, which is unusual for me. I cannot think of what to call it. Here we go.

Today is the one year "anniversary" (not a good word to describe, but...) of my wife's death. (as an aside, I have noticed no one seems to use death, or died. or dead when referring to a family member or loved one. Instead they use passed on, passed away, or some even more flowery synonym or euphemism, but that is probably a post for my other blog. My wife died. The use of a euphemism doesn't diminish the pain or the reality. If I offend anyone, go read another blog. But I digress...)
.
I have extremely mixed emotions today, none of them really good. Sadness and grief are a big part of it; but to be fair, guilt is still a large part of what I feel. You might be thinking one thing, but let me explain. Just after my wife's death (I was going to write "passing" but after the above it didn't seem real), I was wracked with guilt and remorse over some of the things I wish I had done, or said. I do not really regret many of the things I did do, thankfully; but I do have regrets. It is like the famous quotes:

Regret for the things we did can be tempered by time; it is regret for the things we did not do that is inconsolable - Sydney J. Harris

or

When you look back on your life, you'll regret the things you didn't do more than the ones you did. - H. Jackson Brown, Jr.

My wife and I tried to DO as much as we could in the years after her diagnosis. She wanted to go on a cruise with her sister and we did, along with another one a little over a year later. Then we did another one a year and a half later with my youngest daughter. I know she would have rather have done the cruises "whole" and able to partake of more of the activities, but I also know she enjoyed them a LOT. In fact, we might have been better at doing the BIG things (like the cruises, or taking her to Florida) than the smaller things. Those smaller things are what eat at me. It is very sad for me to write this (I will with hope of catharsis), but one of the things she wanted to do was to go to a Russell Stover outlet that is about an hour from here. Now, in the scheme of things, that is not a real difficult request. But, add in the fact of a wheelchair, bathroom issues (see earlier posts), no good wheelchair access at the shopping center the outlet is located in, and my overall exhaustion for most of the time; and it seemed like a HUGE problem to me. I denied her of that trip many times over the months prior to her death. Looking back at it now, I was selfish and foolish. That two hour+ journey might have brought her immeasurable joy for a little effort. There are other regrets similar to that. None big, but that is what makes them so painful.

I wrote some emotional stuff a year ago. Somewhere in there amongst those lines are some words about "doing" and having no regrets. I implore anyone reading this to do what you can if you are faced with a grim future or diagnosis. It actually is pretty good advice for anyone, anytime. I need to heed my own advice, but the healer is always the worst patient.

I will end this with a poem. In the spirit of disclosure, this is actually a one line thing I wrote over forty years ago (before I even met my wife) that I turned into a song for her later. I will not sing for you, but here are the words: (the second verse is chilling to me as I wrote this many, many years ago)

Always will my love for you
remain inside my heart.
No matter where you go
or how long that we're apart.
The promise that I left you with
forever echoes in my ears...I'll need you always.

You were gone one lonesome day

and though I'd told myself before
you'd have to leave me soon
you couldn't stay with me much more.
Still I listen for your laugh,
your smile's forever frozen in my mind...I'll need you always.
                    "THE" 1971 1982

I cannot envision a time that I will not miss her so very much.
RIP - Carol Condon Poole - 09/30/54 - 05/30/11

Now for a piece of trivia to go along with this. My wife died on her
mother's birthday and on Memorial Day weekend. That also makes
things a bit more difficult. My oldest son and I, being USA Men's
soccer fans, decided to go to a international friendly match with
Scotland. The game was in Jacksonville, FL. It was over the Memorial
Day weekend, so I was looking forward to the diversion. Jacksonville is
about a seven-hour drive from Winston-Salem where we were living
at the time, so we had a hotel room in the very southern part of
Georgia just north of Jacksonville. Our exit was around mile marker 7
or so. We got some gas at an exit just before that and headed out. The
car started making a weird bumping sound and was driving weird. We
are on Interstate 95 going about 70 miles per hour when the tread
blew off the tire! The car (with us in it!) did a 180-degree spin on the
interstate, in Memorial Day traffic, and we hit a guard rail totaling the
car. This was on the weekend of the anniversary of Carol's death.
Now, we were lucky in that we were both fine. Also, somehow in
Memorial Day traffic, we crossed over three lanes of traffic -some
sideways, and some backwards – and hit a guardrail, BUT no other
cars were involved. I remember looking out the front window and
seeing what appeared to be a solid wall of cars speeding towards us,
but none hit us. We called a tow truck, rented a car, and went to the
soccer game. I wrote this post in the hotel room after the game. I
have spent the Memorial Day weekends since barricaded indoors.

CHAPTER THIRTY-SEVEN

This post sets itself up. There are two parts:

A Medical & Research Synopsis - Part 1

One of the posts here that continues to get the most hits is the one I did on stem cell therapy. That combined with the fact that I still get emails and questions from patients and caregivers with this and other alphabet diseases has led me to do this post.

I see by the posts on the MSA Facebook pages and other "gathering places" online that the isolation that my wife and I felt when she got her diagnosis is still prevalent in patients and caregivers. The alphabet diseases of the brain are still rare enough that it is still a surprise to find a doctor or nurse that has knowledge of the diseases and their symptoms.

I am going to attempt to outline the what I have found as far as medical knowledge of, pathology of, progression of, and ultimately potential treatments of MSA and related alphabet diseases. I am going to do this in parts, as I have already worked on this one for an hour and barely scratched the surface.

I want to mention again - I am not a medical practitioner of any type. I have a long-standing interest in medicine dating from my childhood combined with a voracious appetite for reading and accumulating knowledge. With my wife's diagnosis of and ultimate death from complications of MSA, I have done even more research into diseases of the human brain concentrating on scientific and medical breakthroughs in this area. So, although I am going to be as accurate and specific as I can be, this is not intended to guide anyone in the treatment, diagnosis, or prognosis of a specific disease. I will share some of my conjecture and opinions, but I will identify them accordingly. I also do not intend to or mean to present this as a scientific paper. I will present this as simply as I can (and as I have to, not being an expert or trained in this area). I am sure I will make mistakes. Do not take anything said here as "gospel". Hopefully this will provide you with some seeds to start your learning process. Most of this I have gotten from the internet, some from scientific journals and textbooks, and some from doctors and researchers I have corresponded with.

A lot of breakthroughs have occurred with brain diseases in the past five to seven years. I know from personal experience, when you and/or a loved one are facing one of these diseases and find it hard to get the information you want, it seems like no one knows anything; but that is not the case.

Actually, the brain itself is still very unknown territory. Doctors and scientists alike are still mystified by the things it does and the processes by which it does them. The diseases that impact the brain are still very much a mystery as well. When one does not know how something is done, figuring out why it is not being done any longer is made almost impossible! One of the "problems" facing researchers into the brain is the fact that a lot of research cannot be done on the human brain for medical and ethical reasons. You cannot dissect a brain without killing the host body. You cannot "try" different procedures on the brain for the same reasons. The human brain is so vastly complex that there is no model outside of the actual brain itself that lends itself to accurate study. Animal research has been of great help in a lot of cases, but the differences in the human brain and its functions from a lab rat's brain is much more dramatic than other systems in the body. The fact that our brain not only performs the physical control center functions of operating movements, processing information, and other animal-like processes; but contains "us", makes any attempt to understand the functions very, very difficult.

I call these diseases "alphabet diseases" for obvious reasons. They are: ALS (Amyotrophic Lateral Sclerosis), CBD (Corticobasal Degeneration), DLB (Dementia with Lewy Bodies), MSA (Multiple System Atrophy), PAF (Pure Autonomic Failure), and PSP (Progressive Supranuclear Palsy). This is not meant to be a complete list, but these all affect the brain and are identified by their initials. They are all now classified as diseases caused by irregular "clumps" of proteins. Depending upon the primary type of this protein they are classified as tauopathies or synucleinopathies. MSA is a synucleinopathy. PSP (and Alzheimer's which I did not mention) is a tauopathies. They are similar in that protein "clumps" aggregate in the brain. The difference is the type of protein that forms these "clumps" - tau or synuclein.

There has been much research into these "clumps" and some

promising results in treating them, at least in vitro (or outside of the body). However, one huge question remains - are these irregular proteins the cause or are they one of the effects? It has been shown in studies that slowing the aggregation of these proteins does slow the progression of these diseases. But again, is it just working on a symptom or a cause? This is a critical question that must be answered prior to any treatments or cures.

Now is a good time to bring up one thing that keeps coming up in comments and posts I see around the web. Although the tauopathies or synucleinopathies all have similarities, and most are called Parkinson's Plus diseases, the pathology of the individual diseases are quite different. As I have already pointed out, the proteins involved in these diseases are distinctly different and divide them into two classes. The areas of the brain affected by the diseases, even with similar symptoms, are different. For example, MSA-P (Parkinson's type with many Parkinson's symptoms and responding to levadopa) is vastly different from Parkinson's. The way I had it explained to me was - in Parkinson's the brain stops producing dopamine. In MSA the receptors for dopamine uptake are degenerating. Compare this to a group communicating by radios. One radio will not transmit, and another will not receive. The result is the same, poor or no communication. The cause is totally different and thus the "cure" would be different. I classify myself as a realistic optimist. I know that research is coming up with chemical compounds and other treatments every day that have a positive effect on one or more of these diseases. I am heartened by these results. However, I also know that a treatment or cure for one does not mean a treatment or cure for another. Any research into the brain and its chemistry is good for all these diseases. As I stated above, there is still so much that is not known about how the brain functions and how these diseases exactly affect the brain, especially in their early stages. So, you can remain positive and be happy when you see a new drug is being tested on Parkinson's patients. But, be cautious as well. One example I will leave you with is pneumonia. Even with all our antibiotics, antiviral agents, vaccines against certain types - pneumonia still kills over 4 million people a year! A "cure" for these alphabet diseases may be a long time coming.

Friday, January 6, 2017
Part 2

http://www.msaawareness.org/ A prime (if not THE prime) location for information - in fact most if not all of the below links can be found on this site as well.

http://rarediseasesnetwork.epi.usf.edu/index.htm
http://www.ataxia.org/
http://www.americanautonomicsociety.org/

And so ended the support posts. I have now noticed that the first link to MSA Awareness is no longer active. Here is a link to the MSA Coalition - https://www.multiplesystematrophy.org/

This is a GREAT resource for information and communication about Multiple System Atrophy.

CHAPTER THIRTY-EIGHT

MORE CREATIVE STUFF

Sometimes when I have a poem pop into my head it is as a song. Other times it has a picture or graphic with it. This is one that was in my head for a while. This one became clear after I heard about the Sandy Hook school shooting the day before.

Saturday, December 15, 2012

Tragedy

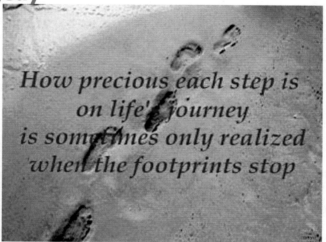

How precious each step is on life's journey is sometimes only realized when the footprints stop

This is something I've had in my mind for quite a while. The horrible killings in Connecticut yesterday prompted me to do it. All the best to those families that were affected by the tragedy.

CHAPTER THIRTY-NINE

COMMUNICATION

When you live with someone for over 38 years you become quite used to them being there. Sharing events, activities, and sights is a normal every day thing; even after they have been gone for almost two years! I was on a trip to Florida for a meeting when I saw something different along the way. I remember saying to myself:

Saturday, February 16, 2013

I have to tell Carol about that

It has been over 20 months since the ambulance came and took my wife away for the last time. Even after that long, it amazes me that I still see or hear things that I think to myself - "oh man, I have to tell Carol (my wife's name) about that. A former boss, friend, and somewhat of a mentor of mine passed away late last year. I just heard about it within the past weeks. The first thing I thought of when I heard was telling my wife, and how amazed she would be.

My wife was from South Florida (by way of the Pittsburgh area, but from age 4 a Florida girl), the Ft. Lauderdale area to be exact. We made many, many trips from N.C. (where I am from, and where we lived as a couple for most of our marriage) to the Ft. Lauderdale area over the years. Then as her mother and a daughter of ours moved to Central Florida - to I-4 and to the Orlando area. I still make the trips to Central Florida quite often. I am writing this from that area, already my second trip this year.

The reason I bring that up is I am very familiar with the wonderful "Main Street East Coast" - I-95, at least from Richmond, Va to Miami. The first trip I took to Florida as a teenager was before most of I-95 was there. As my wife and I made the trips over the years we saw more and more of the highway being completed until it was done (not counting all construction - that never ends!). I know a lot of the exits, a lot of the scenery, a lot of the attractions. I have regular exits that I frequent on my travels. So, when I see something new and interesting it stands out. But as on today's trip, one of my first thoughts is - "I have to tell Carol about that."

So, Carol - you should have seen what I saw! And, David Moore died in late November.

I guess I'll just keep "telling" her. Miss you.

CHAPTER FORTY

STILL TRYING TO HELP

I was struggling to decide what to do with the blog. I was getting hundreds of hits a month and had not posted much new in a while. I felt like I needed to add something.

Sunday, April 7, 2013
Some Thoughts

OK, I shamed myself into writing a post. As I have said now time after time, I am amazed at the people that are still reading this. I feel proud and pleased that the posts that are getting read, for the most part, are those dealing with trying to help others deal with MSA and other alphabet diseases. The most popular post over the past year has been my first about stem cells. I understand the allure, I understand the interest. One of the reasons I wrote the post anyway was after an exhaustive research on my part in looking for something to help my wife. I decided after this research that it was a waste of time and money. I still feel this way. I have had some that have written me saying I am taking away hope. I am maybe guilty of taking away what I (and most experts) feel is false hope. Unless you are in a financial position that $30,000 to $40,000 is not an issue to lose, there appears to be no good reason to try what is a risky, and unproven procedure at this point. My opinion is, it will remain this way for a long time, if not indefinitely. If you have not read the post, in a nutshell (besides being expensive, dangerous, and unproven) to replace cells that are dying without finding, stopping and preventing the reasons for the cell death, at best you are only prolonging the inevitable. There have been some patients that have had the procedure (in China mostly) that have experienced a "remission" of sorts or even an improvement in symptoms for a while after the procedure. I feel this is due to the placebo effect. Now, I realize if you are better, who cares why or how? There are also patients that have died during or immediately after the procedure. I will stand by my comments.

One other issue I will bring up here is one that has been on my mind of late. That is the issue of "awareness". It seems that all my brethren in the MSA family are hell-bent on awareness. I will admit I do not understand the call. If we were among the first groups afflicted with the disease (I was a caregiver to my wife, who died from complications of MSA), I would understand more. There is plenty of awareness among the medical field where it matters; researchers. However, being realistic, with such a small population being affected one cannot expect a full-out assault like the one on polio or smallpox generations ago. I am not trying to be heartless, I am not trying to be a defeatist. I am a realist. Doctors know of Shy-Drager, if not MSA. Doctors are taught OPCA, and other names for the same or similar diseases. The problem is, unless in a large area or a teaching hospital, they may not see an actual patient in their career. When my wife and I went to UNC Neurological Hospital to see a doctor that specializes in MSA (movement disorders is typically where these doctors are categorized), we found he had three other active patients and had treated less than 20 in his career. His department head said that those numbers were typical of the four doctors they had seeing MSA patients. We found this to hold true at Duke University Medical Center, Medical University of South Carolina, and every other hospital we went to.

One of the complaints I hear that I think are driving the awareness calls are concerning how long it takes for a diagnosis. One has to understand, doctors do not want to give this (or similar) diagnoses. Remember there is no cure or treatment. There are no medicines or drugs to "cure" anything. Yes, there are drugs that can help with the symptoms. Most of these are started when those symptoms are noted anyway, regardless of the diagnosis, or lack of. I know from first-hand (or second-hand if you are looking realistically on me as a caregiver, not a patient) experience how frustrating is can be to go from doctor to doctor, test after test, and visit after visit to try to get a handle on what is going on. But, I also remember the devastation when we got the official diagnosis. (I say official because I and to some degree my wife, had already come to that conclusion from our own research) Doctors want to make sure they rule out any other disease which can have similar symptoms, some of which DO have treatments if not cures. Believe me, as hard as the waiting is one does not want to hear the diagnosis of MSA.

On research: there are many fine, wonderful, dedicated, and devoted researchers that are working on finding a cause, treatment, and ultimately a potential cure for MSA and other alphabet diseases of the brain. I feel the greatest results will come from all the research into the brain and its diseases in general. The brain is one of the least understood organs in the human body. To put it in perspective, it essentially cannot do all it does. We can build computers now that can do computations as complex and intricate as the brain. However, we have never come close to building a machine that can do that and all the simultaneous things the brain does AND have self-awareness. The brain is a wondrous, fantastic, intricately homogenized machine that is a problem waiting to happen. The complex, amazing "dance" performed by this organ can be wrecked if just a few "wires are crossed". When dealing with the myriad of brain diseases like MSA, PSP, DLB, HD, PD, ALS, and others, the research is being done at a "grand level". There is still so much we do not know about the brain that a finding from a researcher studying Huntington's Disease may be a breakthrough for MSA or others. It seems to me that as much as we need to support research into MSA specifically, research into any degenerative brain disease benefits the cause.

I wish all reading this well. I hope you are just doing research out of curiosity not because you or you loved one are suffering with MSA. I will remind you that that are pages here that I did covering my wife's symptoms and what steps we took and/or what devices we used to help. They are under the title "Maybe this will help..." There are three pages. They are not truly chronological, as I wrote them as I thought of them. Plus, I can tell you from talking to other MSA patients, although most get the same symptoms they do not come at the same time or in the same order.

This is the post that got me in trouble with the MSA hierarchy for not being all in on "awareness". I just do not see awareness as a great goal. Yes, having medical personnel being aware makes things more convenient and care go a bit smoother in the hospital or ER, but it does not do anything for any patient on its own.

CHAPTER FORTY-ONE

A SONG

As mentioned earlier, poems come to me as songs sometimes. I also am always writing new lyrics (mostly just for myself, I sing them once and forget them) for songs on the radio. This one came to me on day. Carol loved the Village People so I used to sing the opening line to her when the song would come on. Sung to the tune of the Village People's hit "YMCA", I give you:

Tuesday, April 15, 2014

WHY MSA? A theme song

This "song" should be recognizable to most of you. I used to sing the "Why MSA..." part to my wife. I am offering it to the MSA community for whatever.

Hey man, please come gather around.
(I said) Hey girl, come and sit right down.
(I said) All you need to hear what I've found,
There's no cure yet, but we're trying.

Hey man, there's a disease that's around .
(I said) Hey girl, it is tearing us down.
We need you to join us, learn about MSA
And help us to spread the word now.

That's why we're asking you, Why MSA?
We want to know now, Why MSA?

It will knock you down, turn your life around,
You won't be able to do what you feel...

Hey man, are you listening to me?
(I said) Hey girl, I need you really to see
(I said) Hey all, it destroys all your dreams.
But you got to know this one thing!

No one can do it all by themselves.

(I said) Hey man, help us put disease on the shelves.
So learn it, ask Why MSA?
We need your help today.

That's why we're asking you Why MSA?
We want to know now, Why MSA?

I actually contacted the Village People and asked them if they would
be willing to record this version to be used as a fund raiser for MSA
research. I got a very nice reply from them declining. The issue is the
rights to the song. They do not own the song, someone else does.
They basically told me if I would negotiate the legal issues, they would
consider singing it. I never got anywhere with the legal side.

Saturday, May 31, 2014

Battleground

Battleground

We've all fought so many battles
We tend to count the ones we lost.
Trying to build upon our failures
Never adding up the cost.

The big ones seem to be remembered
Fallen soldiers tossed aside.
Forgetting all the minor battles
We should be counting up with pride.

Good days adding to the memories
And the bad days taking toll.
We need to light our way from darkness
Live our lives, not just play a role.

Happiness sure can be elusive
Especially the perfect kind.
We've got to grab onto the goodness
And capture it in our mind.

"THE"
5/31/14

This was the last post on the blog. If you care to see it you can go to
www.livingwithasnowman.blogspot.com.

CHAPTER FORTY-THREE

WRAPPING IT UP

I have pondered over this, the concluding chapter, for a while now. The rest of the book kind of wrote itself. I considered just a short goodbye with some well-wishes and also a long epistle covering life and death. This, I hope, will fall somewhere in the middle.

Through the blog and various support groups I have "met" and "talked with" many surviving family members (the quotes are due to the fact that almost all of these folks are online "friends". We have "met" and "spoken" in chat rooms, emails, messages, etc. Most I have never met in person) I also have been contacted by those that have lost loved ones in other ways that were kind enough to tell me that the blog touched some part of them as well, and some I know in "real life". I have had discussions (with one person in particular – and you know who you are) about the impact of losing a spouse or immediate family member, and the differences between an immediate unexpected death and one that is inevitable due to an illness like MSA or another alphabet disease. It would seem that a "planned" demise would be easier to accept, and not having faced the other; I cannot say for sure, maybe it is. However, one point I have brought up is this: unless your loved one is on life support that is going to be ended – excuse the possibly cold language – by "pulling the plug" or similar, you do not expect the day of death to be THE day of death. My wife and I had a Saturday like most others in the advanced stage of her disease. We went about our routine and just lived the day. I had no idea as I was wheeling her back to get ready for bed that this was the last time I would do so. Because she stopped breathing, we never said our goodbyes; at least not verbally.

It is strange to me that one of the only things that every person on that planet shares with every other – death – is something we do not really discuss. Every person on this earth is going to perish. Now, I am not trying to be morbid, just trying to make a point; we do not discuss death in any depth in most circumstances. I mentioned that Carol and I never really talked about her death. It was just the elephant in the room that we both maneuvered around. I do know that we need to embrace death as inevitable but cherish and enjoy each day of life as a wonder and a blessing.

I want to end with a post from my other blog: www.justsomeposts.blogspot.com. It concerns life as a continuum.

Beginnings, Middles, and Ends; Oh My!

I was thinking how we spend our lives going from beginnings to ends. There is the BIG beginning - BIRTH, and the BIG ending - DEATH. Then LIFE is what happens in the middle. But, life is really a continuum of beginning - middle - end; over and over.

We humans, for the most part, LOVE beginnings. Think about one of our most celebrated personal days - the anniversary of our beginning - our birthday! We document, record, and celebrate other beginnings - baby's first words, first steps, first day of school, first date, first kiss, first car, first job, etc. We have such a love of beginnings that we keep seeking them all through our lives - just substitute NEW for FIRST. We have new jobs, new cars, new clothes, new loves, and so on. We move to new houses and neighborhoods. New is a good substitute for a beginning (and IS one in a way, I have to concede)

It can get somewhat complicated when we get to endings. Think of a graduation. It is called a commencement. To commence is to "begin, to start". We have taken an ending - of school, or at least that portion of school, and made it a beginning - a commencement of another chapter of life. We keep looking for beginnings after the endings. As stated above - we lose a job...YAAAAA we get a NEW JOB! We get a divorce...OH YEAH we get a NEW LOVE (or even NEW LIFE)! We even have a beginning attached to the BIG ending of death - metaphysics and/or religion offer up Heaven or reincarnation.

What I really find amazing is that most of our life is in the middle. Yes, almost every day has the small beginnings of new, but for the most part we are just existing and getting by. (I do not mean to imply that good and evil are not being committed and that people are not accomplishing things, but in a big picture kind of way - the middle is just getting through the days)

It seems to me however, that for all the beginnings and endings - even with the "news" in there - for the most part we live the majority of our lives in between. Every book has a cover and a back - a beginning and end as it were - but if you do not read the middle all books are basically the same.

IN THE END - I THINK WE FIND IT IS THE MIDDLE THAT MATTERS!

"THE" 4/2017

I wish each and every one of you, as well as all your loved ones, a wonderful life! Enjoy the middle, however much of it there is.

Scott Poole, Dr.B.A.

Made in the USA
Columbia, SC
17 October 2020